Kaplan Publishing are constantly finding new ways to make a difference to your studies and our exciting online resources really do offer something different to students looking for exam success.

This book comes with free MyKaplan online ~~resources~~ ...at you can study anytime, anywhere. **This fr~~...~~ resource is not sold separately and is included in the price of the book.**

Having purchased this book, you have access to the following online study materials:

CONTENT	AAT	
	Text	Kit
iPaper version of the book	✓	✓
Progress tests with instant answers	✓	
Mock assessments online	✓	✓
Material updates	✓	✓

How to access your online resources

Kaplan Financial students will already have a MyKaplan account and these extra resources will be available to you online. You do not need to register again, as this process was completed when you enrolled. If you are having problems accessing online materials, please ask your course administrator.

If you are already a registered MyKaplan user go to www.MyKaplan.co.uk and log in. Select the 'add a book' feature and enter the ISBN number of this book and the unique pass key at the bottom of this card. Then click 'finished' or 'add another book'. You may add as many books as you have purchased from this screen.

If you purchased through Kaplan Flexible Learning or via the Kaplan Publishing website you will automatically receive an e-mail invitation to MyKaplan. Please register your details using this email to gain access to your content. If you do not receive the e-mail or book content, please contact Kaplan Flexible Learning.

If you are a new user register at www.MyKaplan.co.uk and click on the link contained in the email we sent you to activate your account. Then select the 'add a book' feature, enter the ISBN number of this book and the unique pass key at the bottom of this card. Then click 'finished' or 'add another book'.

Your Code and Information

This code can only be used once for the registration of one book online. This registration and your online content will expire when the final sittings for the examinations covered by this book have taken place. Please allow one hour from the time you submit your book details for us to process your request.

Please scratch the film to access your MyKaplan code.

Please be aware that this code is case-sensitive and you will need to include the dashes within the passcode, but not when entering the ISBN. For further technical support, please visit www.MyKaplan.co.uk

Professional Examinations

AQ2013 Level 2

Basic Costing

REVISION KIT

KAPLAN

PUBLISHING

British Library Cataloguing-in-Publication Data

A catalogue record for this book is available from the British Library.

Published by:

Kaplan Publishing UK

Unit 2 The Business Centre

Molly Millar's Lane

Wokingham

Berkshire

RG41 2QZ

ISBN: 978-1-78415-354-0

© Kaplan Financial Limited, 2015

Printed and bound in Great Britain

CONTENTS

	Page
Index to questions and answers	v
Exam technique	xi
Paper specific information	xiii
Kaplan's recommended revision approach	xv
Practice questions	1
Answers to practice questions	49
Mock exam questions	83
Mock exam answers	95

Features in this exam kit

In addition to providing a wide ranging bank of real exam style questions, we have also included in this kit:

- Paper specific information and advice on exam technique.

- Our recommended approach to make your revision for this particular subject as effective as possible.

You will find a wealth of other resources to help you with your studies on the AAT website:

www.aat.org.uk/

Quality and accuracy are of the utmost importance to us so if you spot an error in any of our products, please send an email to mykaplanreporting@kaplan.com with full details, or follow the link to the feedback form in MyKaplan.

Our Quality Co-ordinator will work with our technical team to verify the error and take action to ensure it is corrected in future editions

INDEX TO QUESTIONS AND ANSWERS

		Page number	
		Question	Answer
COST CLASSIFICATION			
Financial and Management Accounting			
1	FAMA	1	49
2	Financial and management	1	49
3	MAFA	2	50
4	Features	2	50
Cost and profit centres			
5	Jeremy	2	50
6	Print plc	3	50
7	Hooch plc	3	51
Classifying costs by element (materials, labour or overheads)			
8	VVV Ltd	3	51
9	Trip Ltd	4	51
10	FRUWT Ltd	4	51
11	Martin	4	52
Classifying costs by nature (direct or indirect)			
12	Russell	5	52
13	Russett Ltd	5	52
14	Scotland Ltd	5	52
15	Direct or Indirect	6	52
16	Direct costs	6	53
Classifying costs by function (production, administration or selling and distribution)			
17	Noogle Ltd	6	53
18	Heaving Ltd	7	53
19	Korma plc	7	54
20	James	7	54
Classifying costs by behaviour (fixed, variable or semi-variable)			
21	Quark Ltd	8	54
22	Morn Ltd	8	54
23	Stepped fixed cost	8	55
24	Braetak Ltd	9	55
25	Odo Ltd	9	55
26	Definitions	9	55
27	Match a graph	10	56

		Page number	
		Question	Answer
COST CODING			
28	Bytes Ltd	10	56
29	Hero Ltd	11	56
30	Villain Ltd	12	56
31	Nayulz Ltd	12	57
32	Jumper Ltd	13	57
33	Greenfingers	14	57
COST BEHAVIOUR			
Calculation questions			
34	Hulk plc	14	57
35	Banner plc	15	58
36	Norton plc	15	58
Narrative style questions			
37	Bungle plc	15	58
38	TF	16	59
39	Fixed or variable	16	59
40	FOV	16	59
41	VOF	16	59
42	Storm	17	59
43	Rogue	17	60
44	Gambit	17	60
Cost cards, total costs and unit costs			
45	Jeepers Ltd	17	60
46	Braniac Ltd	18	60
47	Gloria Ltd	18	61
48	Bizarro Ltd	19	61
49	Vinny Ltd	19	61
50	Darkseid Ltd	20	61
51	Doomsday Ltd	20	61
52	Olsen Ltd	20	62
53	Flakeaway Ltd	21	62
54	Coronation Ltd	21	62
55	Luthor Ltd	22	62
Manufacturing Accounts			
56	Joker Ltd	22	63
57	Tut Ltd	23	63
58	Riddler Ltd	24	64
59	Clocking Ltd	24	64
60	Bookworm Ltd	25	65
61	Multi	25	65

KAPLAN PUBLISHING

		Page number	
		Question	Answer

COSTING FOR INVENTORY AND WORK-IN-PROGRESS

Narrative style questions

62	Bobble Ltd	26	65
63	Lint Ltd	26	66
64	Fluff Ltd	26	66
65	Fido Ltd	27	66
66	Truffeaux Ltd	27	66
67	Stocky Ltd	27	67

Identification of inventory valuation method

68	Epic Ltd	28	67
69	Awesome Ltd	28	67
70	Amazing Ltd	29	68

Inventory cards

71	Stone Ltd	29	68
72	Natal Ltd	30	68
73	Gandalf Ltd	30	69
74	Grundy Ltd	31	69
75	Lobo Ltd	31	70
76	Zod Ltd	32	70

COSTING FOR LABOUR

Narrative-style questions

77	Nulab Ltd	32	71
78	Lu Ltd	33	71
79	Mandela Ltd	33	71
80	Perres Ltd	33	71
81	Tevez Ltd	34	72
82	Berdych Ltd	34	72
83	Soderling Ltd	34	72
84	Murray Ltd	34	72
85	Owen Ltd	35	72
86	Piecework	35	73

| | | Page number | |
		Question	Answer
Calculating labour costs			
87	Mutant Ltd	35	73
88	Phoenix Ltd	36	73
89	Kahn Ltd	36	73
90	Enterprise Ltd	36	73
91	SGC Ltd	37	74
92	Gothic Ltd	37	74
93	Avengers Ltd	37	74
94	Draco Ltd	38	74
95	Quagga plc	38	74
96	JLA plc	38	75
97	Injustice Ltd	39	75
98	Greenwood Ltd	39	75

SPREADSHEETS AND VARIANCES

Narrative questions			
99	Various Ltd	39	75
100	Spreadsheets	40	76
101	Stuff Ltd	40	76
Variance spreadsheet questions			
102	Erebor Ltd	41	76
103	Moria Ltd	42	77
104	Wyedale Ltd	43	78
105	Belegost Ltd	43	78
106	Ivan Ltd	44	79
107	Bluebell Ltd	45	79
Spreadsheet format questions			
108	Elves Ltd	46	80
109	Hobbit plc	47	81
110	Smaug plc	48	81

MOCK EXAM		
Questions	83	
Answers		95

PAPER ENHANCEMENTS

We have added the following enhancements to the answers in this exam kit:

Key answer tips

Some answers include key answer tips to help your understanding of each question.

Tutorial note

Some answers include more tutorial notes to explain some of the technical points in more detail.

EXAM TECHNIQUE

- **Do not skip any of the material** in the syllabus.

- **Read each question** *very* carefully.

- **Double-check your answer** before committing yourself to it.

- Answer **every** question – if you do not know an answer to a multiple choice question or true/false question, you don't lose anything by guessing. Think carefully before you **guess**.

- If you are answering a multiple-choice question, **eliminate first those answers that you know are wrong**. Then choose the most appropriate answer from those that are left.

- **Don't panic** if you realise you've answered a question incorrectly. Getting one question wrong will not mean the difference between passing and failing

Computer-based exams – tips

- Do not attempt a CBA until you have **completed all study material** relating to it.

- On the AAT website there is a CBA demonstration. It is **ESSENTIAL** that you attempt this before your real CBA. You will become familiar with how to move around the CBA screens and the way that questions are formatted, increasing your confidence and speed in the actual exam.

- Be sure you understand how to use the **software** before you start the exam. If in doubt, ask the assessment centre staff to explain it to you.

- Questions are **displayed on the screen** and answers are entered using keyboard and mouse. At the end of the exam, you are given a certificate showing the result you have achieved.

- In addition to the traditional multiple-choice question type, CBAs will also contain **other types of questions**, such as number entry questions, drag and drop, true/false, pick lists or drop down menus or hybrids of these.

- In some CBAs you will have to type in complete computations or written answers.

- You need to be sure you **know how to answer questions** of this type before you sit the exam, through practice.

PAPER SPECIFIC INFORMATION

THE EXAM

FORMAT OF THE ASSESSMENT

Expect to see 17 tasks in the assessment, many of which will be split into more than one section. The tasks will cover all of the learning outcomes from the syllabus.

Task	Maximum marks	Title for topics within task range
1	8	Statements, financial and management accounting
2	8	Classifying costs by element, classifying costs by nature
3	8	Classifying costs by function, classifying costs by behaviour
4	6	Cost coding
5	6	Cost coding
6	9	Cost behaviour calculation, classifying costs by behaviour
7	8	Cost behaviour – narrative style, cost cards, total costs and unit costs
8	14	Manufacturing accounts
9	9	Identification of inventory valuation method, inventory cards
10	9	Inventory cards
11	8	Labour – narrative style, calculating labour costs
12	8	Labour – calculating labour costs
13	9	Labour – calculating labour costs
14	12	Spreadsheet format
15	8	Spreadsheet narrative
16	12	Variance spreadsheet, spreadsheet format
17	8	Variance spreadsheet, spreadsheet format

TIME ALLOWED

2 hours

PASS MARK

The pass mark for all AAT CBAs is 70%.

 Always keep your eye on the clock and make sure you attempt all questions!

DETAILED SYLLABUS

The detailed syllabus and study guide written by the AAT can be found at:

www.aat.org.uk/

KAPLAN'S RECOMMENDED REVISION APPROACH

QUESTION PRACTICE IS THE KEY TO SUCCESS

Success in professional examinations relies upon you acquiring a firm grasp of the required knowledge at the tuition phase. In order to be able to do the questions, knowledge is essential.

However, the difference between success and failure often hinges on your exam technique on the day and making the most of the revision phase of your studies.

The **Kaplan textbook** is the starting point, designed to provide the underpinning knowledge to tackle all questions. However, in the revision phase, poring over text books is not the answer.

The Kaplan workbook helps you consolidate your knowledge and understanding and is a useful tool to check whether you can remember key topic areas.

Kaplan pocket notes are designed to help you quickly revise a topic area, however you then need to practise questions. There is a need to progress to exam style questions as soon as possible, and to tie your exam technique and technical knowledge together.

The importance of question practice cannot be over-emphasised.

The recommended approach below is designed by expert tutors in the field, in conjunction with their knowledge of the examiner and the specimen assessment.

You need to practise as many questions as possible in the time you have left.

OUR AIM

Our aim is to get you to the stage where you can attempt exam questions confidently, to time, in a closed book environment, with no supplementary help (i.e. to simulate the real examination experience).

Practising your exam technique is also vitally important for you to assess your progress and identify areas of weakness that may need more attention in the final run up to the examination.

In order to achieve this we recognise that initially you may feel the need to practice some questions with open book help.

Good exam technique is vital.

THE KAPLAN BCST REVISION PLAN

Stage 1: Assess areas of strengths and weaknesses

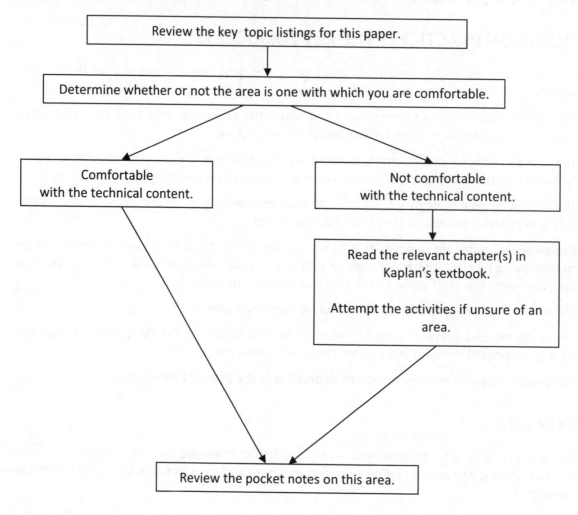

Stage 2: Practise questions

Follow the order of revision of topics as presented in this kit and attempt the questions in the order suggested.

Try to avoid referring to text books, notes and the model answer until you have completed your attempt.

Review your attempt with the model answer and assess how much of the answer you achieved.

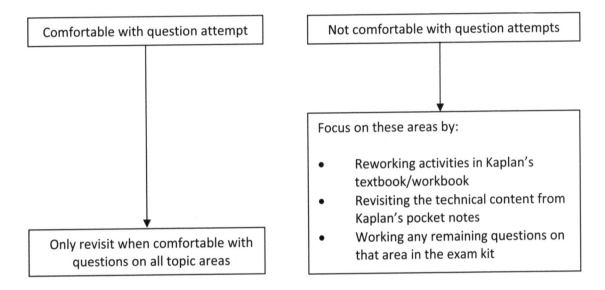

Stage 3: Final pre-exam revision

We recommend that you **attempt at least one two hour mock examination** containing a set of previously unseen exam standard questions.

Attempt the mock CBA online in timed, closed book conditions to simulate the real exam experience.

Section 1

PRACTICE QUESTIONS

COST CLASSIFICATION

FINANCIAL AND MANAGEMENT ACCOUNTING

1   FAMA

The table below lists some of the characteristics of financial accounting and management accounting systems.

Indicate two characteristics for each system by putting a tick in the relevant column of the table below:

Characteristic	Financial accounting	Management accounting
• Have to be produced annually.		
• Analyses historic events to help produce forecasts.		
• Is always produced using accounting standards.		
• Is produced on an ad hoc basis when required.		

2   FINANCIAL AND MANAGEMENT

The table below lists some of the characteristics of financial accounting and management accounting systems.

Indicate two characteristics for each system by putting a tick in the relevant column of the table below:

Characteristic	Financial accounting	Management accounting
• Must be presented as specified by the Companies Act and accounting standards.		
• Helps managers run the business on a day-to-day basis.		
• Used as the basis for the calculation of the organisation's tax charge.		
• Can include anything that managers feel is useful for the business.		

3   MAFA

The table below lists some of the characteristics of financial accounting and management accounting systems.

Indicate two characteristics for each system by putting a tick in the relevant column of the table below:

Characteristic	Management accounting	Financial accounting
• It is based on past events. • Its purpose is to provide information for managers. • It is based on future events. • It complies with company law and accounting rules.		

4   FEATURES

The table below lists some features typical of financial accounting and management accounting systems.

Indicate which feature applies to which system by putting a tick in the relevant column of the table below:

Feature	Financial accounting	Management accounting
• Analysis of profit by cost centre.		✓
• Statement of profit or loss using format as dictated by accounting standards and company law.	✓	
• Cash flow forecasts.		✓
• Cost per unit calculation.		✓

COST AND PROFIT CENTRES

5   JEREMY

Jeremy operates a business that bakes bread. These are made in a small bakery and then sent to Jeremy's shop, where they are sold. Jeremy also has a small office where all of the administration is undertaken.

Identify whether the following departments are likely to be profit or cost centres by putting a tick in the relevant column of the table below:

Department	Cost centre	Profit centre
• Bakery	✓	
• Shop	✓	✓
• Office	✓	✓

6 PRINT PLC

Print plc is a large company that prints and sells books. It is split into three divisions – binding, shops and marketing. The binding department prints the books. These are then either transferred to Print's chain of shops where they are sold to the public, or sold direct from the binding department to corporate clients. The marketing department produces all of Print's advertising.

Identify whether the following departments are likely to be profit or cost centres by putting a tick in the relevant column of the table below:

Department	Cost centre	Profit centre
• Binding	V →	
• Shops	V →	
• Marketing	←	✓

7 HOOCH PLC

Identify whether the following definitions are of be profit, cost, or investment centres by putting a tick in the relevant column of the table below:

Department	Cost centre	Profit centre	Investment centre
• Hooch's manager has no responsibility for income or asset purchases and disposals.	∨		
• Hooch's manager is assessed on the profitability of their department, as well as how effectively they have controlled their assets.		✗	∨
• Hooch's manager is responsible for income and expenditure of their department only.		∨	✗

CLASSIFYING COSTS BY ELEMENT (MATERIALS, LABOUR OR OVERHEADS)

8 VVV LTD

VVV Ltd manufactures toy planes.

Classify the following costs by element (materials, labour or overheads) by putting a tick in the relevant column of the table below:

Cost	Materials	Labour	Overheads
• Paint used on the planes.	V		
• Depreciation of the machines used in the factory.			✓
• Oil used on the machines in the factory.			✓
• Salary of worker assembling the planes.		✓	

9 TRIP LTD

Trip Ltd is a company that provides travel insurance.

Classify the following costs by element (materials, labour or overheads) by putting a tick in the relevant column of the table below:

Cost	Materials	Labour	Overheads
• Wages of the insurance clerks dealing with claims.		✓	
• Rent of the office.			✓
• Paper used to print off insurance policies.	✓		
• Salary of the office manager.		✓	✗

10 FRUWT LTD

FRUWT Ltd manufactures and sells fruit juice.

Classify the following costs by element (materials, labour or overheads) by putting a tick in the relevant column of the table below:

Cost	Materials	Labour	Overheads
• Purchase of fruit for juicing.	✓		
• Electricity used by juicing machines.			✓
• Water added to the juice before sale.	✓		
• Wages of staff operating juicing machinery.		✓	

11 MARTIN

Martin provides legal services in his home town.

Classify the following costs by element (materials, labour or overheads) by putting a tick in the relevant column of the table below:

Cost	Materials	Labour	Overheads
• Stationery used in Martin's court cases.	✓		
• Wages of Martin's secretary.		✓	
• Water rates for Martin's office.			✓
• Cost of training courses taken by Martin.			✓

CLASSIFYING COSTS BY NATURE (DIRECT OR INDIRECT)

12 RUSSELL

Russell runs a newspaper.

Classify the following costs by nature (direct or indirect) by putting a tick in the relevant column of the table below:

Cost	Direct	Indirect
• Paper used in the newspapers.	✓	
• Wages of warehouse staff.	✗	✓
• Heat and light for head office.		✓
• Ink used in printing the newspapers.	✓	

13 RUSSETT LTD

Russett Ltd is in business as a tablet computer manufacturer.

Classify the following costs by nature (direct or indirect) by putting a tick in the relevant column of the table below:

Cost	Direct	Indirect
• Glass used to make tablets.	✓	
• Insurance of factory.		✓
• Wages of workers assembling tablets.	✓	
• Cost of entertaining corporate clients.		✓

14 SCOTLAND LTD

Scotland Ltd makes sports clothing.

Classify the following costs by nature (direct or indirect) by putting a tick in the relevant column of the table below:

Cost	Direct	Indirect
• Cleaners' wages.		✓
• Advertising expense.	✗	✓
• Material used in production.	✓	
• Production manager's wages.	✓ →	
• Machinist wages.	✓	

15   DIRECT OR INDIRECT

Classify the following costs by nature (direct or indirect) by putting a tick in the relevant column of the table below:

Cost	Direct	Indirect
• Chargeable hour for a lawyer.	✓	
• Machine hire for a building contractor in a long term contract.	✓	
• Electricity for a garden centre.	✓ →·	
• Audit fee for a restaurant.		✓

16   DIRECT COSTS ARE CONVENTIONALLY DEEMED TO:

A   be constant in total when activity levels alter

B   be constant per unit of activity

C   vary per unit of activity where activity levels alter

D   vary in total when activity levels remain constant

CLASSIFYING COSTS BY FUNCTION (PRODUCTION, ADMINISTRATION OR SELLING AND DISTRIBUTION)

17   NOOGLE LTD

Noogle Ltd produces microwaveable ready meals.

Classify the following costs by function (production, administration, or selling and distribution) by putting a tick in the relevant column of the table below:

Cost	Production	Administration	Selling and distribution
• Purchases of plastic for ready meal containers.	✓		
• Depreciation of sales department's delivery lorries.			✓
• Insurance of office computers.		✓	
• Salaries of production workers.	✓		

18 HEAVING LTD

Heaving Ltd produces exercise equipment.

Classify the following costs by function (production, administration, or selling and distribution) by putting a tick in the relevant column of the table below:

Cost	Production	Administration	Selling and distribution
• Paper used to print off sales invoices.		✓	~~✓~~
• Metal used to make weights and bars.	✓		
• Depreciation of sales person's vehicle.			✓
• Repairs to machine in factory.	✓		

19 KORMA PLC

Classify the following costs by function (production, administration, selling and distribution or finance) by putting a tick in the relevant column of the table below:

Cost	Production	Administration	Selling and distribution	Finance
• Direct materials.	✓			
• Sales director salary.			✓	
• Head office printer ink.		✓		
• Direct labour.	✓			
• Bank charges.				✓

20 JAMES

James makes false teeth.

Classify the following costs by function (production, administration, selling and distribution or finance) by putting a tick in the relevant column of the table below:

Cost	Production	Administration	Selling and distribution	Finance
• Salary of receptionist.		✓		
• Plastic used in false teeth.	✓			
• Stationery provided to all departments.		✓		
• Interest on James' bank overdraft.				✓
• Electricity for James' factory.	✓			

CLASSIFYING COSTS BY BEHAVIOUR (FIXED, VARIABLE OR SEMI-VARIABLE)

21 QUARK LTD

Quark Ltd runs a bar.

Classify the following costs by their behaviour (fixed, variable, or semi-variable) by putting a tick in the relevant column of the table below:

Cost	Fixed	Variable	Semi-variable
• Bar manager's salary.	✓		
• Alcohol used to make drinks.		✓	
• Rent of bar.	✓		
• Telephone costs, including standard line rental charge.			✓

22 MORN LTD

Morn Ltd is a manufacturer of chairs and stools.

Classify the following costs by their behaviour (fixed, variable, or semi-variable) by putting a tick in the relevant column of the table below:

Cost	Fixed	Variable	Semi-variable
• Wood used in production.		✓	
• Advertising manager's salary.	✓		
• Electricity costs which include a standing charge.			✓
• Labour costs paid on a piecework basis.		✓	

23 STEPPED FIXED COST

Which of the following would usually be classed as a stepped fixed cost?

A   Supervisor's wages

B   Raw materials

C   Rates

D   Telephone

KAPLAN PUBLISHING

24   BRAETAK LTD

Classify the following costs by their behaviour (fixed, variable, or semi-variable) by putting a tick in the relevant column of the table below:

Cost	Fixed	Variable	Semi-variable
• Rent of an office building.	✓		
• Wages of production staff paid on an hourly basis.		✓	
• Wages of production staff paid by a piece rate method.		✓	
• Sales staff paid a basic wage plus commission for each unit sold.			✓

25   ODO LTD

Odo Ltd is a manufacturer of clothes.

Classify the following costs by their behaviour (fixed, variable, or semi-variable) by putting a tick in the relevant column of the table below:

Cost	Fixed	Variable	Semi-variable
• Material used in the production process.		✓	
• Safety review fee for the year.	✓		
• Electricity costs which include a standing charge.			✓
• Labour costs paid on a per unit basis.		✓	

26   DEFINITIONS

Identify the following costs by their behaviour (fixed, variable, or semi-variable) by putting a tick in the relevant column of the table below:

Behaviour	Fixed	Variable	Semi-variable	Stepped cost
• This type of cost increases in direct proportion to the amount of units produced.		✓		
• This type of cost has a fixed and a variable element.			✓	
• This type of cost remains constant despite changes in output.	✓			
• This type of cost is fixed within a certain range of output.				✓

27 MATCH A GRAPH

Match a graph to each of the following costs by labelling each graph with a letter (A–E):

(a) Variable cost per unit

(b) Total fixed cost

(c) Stepped fixed costs

(d) Total variable cost

(e) Semi-variable cost

Note: Each graph may relate to more than one cost.

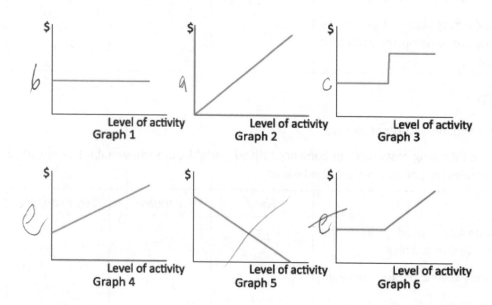

COST CODING

28 BYTES LTD

Bytes Limited operates an IT consultancy business and uses a coding system for its elements of cost (materials, labour or overheads) and then further classifies each element by nature (direct or indirect cost) as below:

So, for example, the code for direct materials is A100.

Element of cost	Code	Nature of cost	Code
Materials	A	Direct	100
		Indirect	200
Labour	B	Direct	100
		Indirect	200
Overheads	C	Direct	100
		Indirect	200

Code the following costs, extracted from invoices and payroll, using the table below:

Cost	Code
• Salary of trainee IT consultant.	B 100 ✓
• Planning costs to renew lease of the office.	C 200 ✓
• Wages of the office manager.	B 200 ✓
• Cleaning materials used by cleaner.	A 200 ✓

29 HERO LTD

Hero Ltd, a manufacturer of superhero costumes, uses a numerical coding structure based on one profit centre and three cost centres as outlined below. Each code has a sub-code so each transaction will be coded as ***/***

Profit/cost centre	Code	Sub-classification	Sub-code
Sales	115	Women's costumes	085
		Men's costumes	095
Production	225	Direct cost	110
		Indirect cost	115
Administration	485	Direct cost	220
		Indirect cost	230
Selling and distribution	760	Direct cost	320
		Indirect cost	340

Code the following revenue and expense transactions, which have been extracted from purchase invoices, sales invoices and payroll, using the table below:

Transaction	Code
• Cost of major advertising campaign.	760/340 ✓
• Oil for machinery in factory.	225/115 ✓
• Silk used in manufacturing of costumes.	225/110 ✓
• Insurance of head office.	485/230 ✓
• Sale of women's costumes to a supermarket chain.	115/085 ✓
• Wages paid to delivery van drivers.	760/340 ?

30   VILLAIN LTD

Villain Ltd, a mining company, uses a numerical coding structure based on one profit centre and three cost centres as outlined below. Each code has a sub-code so each transaction will be coded as ***/***

Profit/cost centre	Code	Sub-classification	Sub-code
Revenue	011	Gold sales	100
		Other sales	200
Production	015	Direct Cost	100
		Indirect Cost	200
Administration	019	Direct Cost	100
		Indirect Cost	200
Selling and distribution	024	Direct Cost	100
		Indirect Cost	200

Code the following revenue and expense transactions, which have been extracted from purchase invoices, sales invoices and payroll, using the table below:

Transaction	Code
• Petrol used to run drilling machinery.	015/200 ✓
• Sale of silver to a jewellery manufacturer.	011/200 ✓
• Replacement of worn out drilling machinery parts.	015/200 ✓
• Depreciation of fleet of delivery lorries.	024/200 ✓
• Salary of finance director.	019/200 ?
• Sale of gold to an electronics company.	011/100 ✓

31   NAYULZ LTD

Nayulz Limited operates a chain of nail salons across Europe and America.

Code the following transactions for the project, using the table below. Each transaction should have a five-character code.

Activity	Code	Nature of cost	Sub-code
Investments	IN	External	100
		Internal	110
Revenues	RE	Europe	225
		America	228
Costs	CO	Material	315
		Labour	318
		Overheads	325

Code the following costs, extracted from invoices and payroll, using the table below:

Cost	Code
• Income earned from salons in New York City, America.	RE 228 ✓
• Bank loans raised to open a new store in London.	IN 100 ✓
• Nail polish purchased for use in salon.	CO 315 ✓
• Heat and light for salon.	CO 325 ✓
• Nayulz funds invested in new project.	IN 110 ✓

32 JUMPER LTD

Jumper Ltd manufactures a range of different items of clothing, which it sells to various types of organisation.

The company analyses sales using an alphanumeric coding system depending on the type of clothing being sold, as well as the type of organisation the clothes are being sold to.

Type of clothing	Code
Trousers	TRS
Jumpers	KNI
Coats	MCN

Sale made to:	Code
Individuals	315
Shops	425
Offices	515
Factories	635

For example, sale of coats to a factory would be coded as MCN/635

Code the following transactions, using the table below:

Sale	Code
• Sale of one jumper to Mrs S. Wooley.	KNI/315 ✓
• Sale of protective trousers to a factory in London.	TRS/635 ✓
• Sale of large coats to an office in Birmingham.	MCN/515 ✓
• Sale of woolen jumpers to a shop in Halifax.	KNI/425 ✓
• Sale of four coats to Mr A. West.	MCN/315 ✓
• Sale of three hundred trousers to a shop in Manchester.	TRS/425 ✓

33   GREENFINGERS

Greenfingers Ltd runs a garden centre and uses a coding system for its transactions.

Code the following transactions, using the table below. Each transaction must have a five character code.

Element of cost	Code	Nature of cost	Code
Investments	IN	External	515
		Internal	615
Revenues	RV	Plants	770
		Other	795
Costs	CS	Material	880
		Labour	890
		Overheads	900

Code the following costs, extracted from invoices and payroll, using the table below:

Cost	Code
• Purchase of seeds used to grow plants for resale.	CS880
• External loans for investment in new greenhouses.	IN 515
• Wages of gardeners who maintain the plants to be sold.	CS 890
• Sales of food and drink.	RV 795

COST BEHAVIOUR

CALCULATION QUESTIONS

34   HULK PLC

Identify the type of cost behaviour (fixed, variable or semi-variable) described in each statement by putting a tick in the relevant column of the table below:

Statement	Fixed	Variable	Semi-variable
• Costs are £37,500 when 7,500 units are made and £62,500 when 12,500 units are made.		✓	
• Costs are £2 per unit when 7,500 units are made and £1.20 per unit when 12,500 units are made.	✓		
• Costs are £50,000 when 7,500 units are made and £80,000 when 12,500 units are made.			✓

35 BANNER PLC

Identify the type of cost behaviour (fixed, variable or semi-variable) described in each statement by putting a tick in the relevant column of the table below:

Statement	Fixed	Variable	Semi-variable
• Costs are £5,000 plus £45 per unit, regardless of the number of units made.			
• Costs are £5,000 when 300 units are made and £5,000 when 600 units are made.	✓		
• Costs are £35 per unit regardless of the number of units made.			

36 NORTON PLC

Identify the type of cost behaviour (fixed, variable or semi-variable) described in each statement by putting a tick in the relevant column of the table below:

Statement	Fixed	Variable	Semi-variable
• Costs are £50,000 in total regardless of the number of units made.	✓		
• Costs are £50,000 in total when 2,500 units are made and £80,000 when 4,000 units are made.			
• Costs are £7 per unit when 1,000 units are made and £6 per unit when 2,000 units are made.			

NARRATIVE STYLE QUESTIONS

37 BUNGLE LTD

Bungle Ltd usually produces 9,000 units but is planning to increase production to 14,000 units during the next period.

Identify the following statements as either true or false by putting a tick in the relevant column of the table below:

Statement	True	False
• Total variable costs will decrease.		✓
• Total fixed costs will remain the same.	✓	
• The variable cost per unit will remain the same.	✓	
• The fixed cost per unit will increase.		✓

38 TF

Identify the following statements as either true or false by putting a tick in the relevant column of the table below:

Statement	True	False
• Variable costs change directly with changes in activity.	✓	
• Fixed costs change directly with changes in activity.		✓
• Stepped costs are fixed within a set range of output.	✓	

39 FIXED OR VARIABLE

Identify the following costs as either fixed or variable by putting a tick in the relevant column of the table below:

Cost	Fixed	Variable
• Direct materials.		✓
• Power used in production machinery.		✓
• Training costs for new employees in production.	✓	
• Insurance for sales cars.	✓	
• Insurance for machinery.	✓	
• Sales commission.		✓

40 FOV

Identify the following costs as either fixed or variable by putting a tick in the relevant column of the table below:

Cost	Fixed	Variable
• Piecework wages paid to factory workers.		✓
• Salaries paid to company directors.	✓	
• Annual payment for cleaning of air conditioning units.	✓	

41 VOF

VOF is a company that prints magazines and newspapers.

Identify the following costs as either fixed or variable by putting a tick in the relevant column of the table below:

Cost	Fixed	Variable
• Annual salaries paid to factory managers.	✓	
• Hourly wages paid to factory workers.		✓
• Colour ink used to print magazines.		✓

42 STORM

Indicate whether each of the following costs is an overhead or not by putting a tick in the relevant column of the table below:

	Overhead?	
Cost	Yes	No
• Labour cost of workers who assemble the product.		✓
• Insurance cost of factory where product is assembled.	✓	
• Electricity for machinery.	✓	

43 ROGUE

Indicate whether each of the following costs is an overhead or not by putting a tick in the relevant column of the table below:

	Overhead?	
Cost	Yes	No
• Labour cost of cleaning staff in a factory.	✓	
• Depreciation of delivery vans.	✓	
• Cost of materials used to build the product.		✓

44 GAMBIT

Indicate whether each of the following costs is an overhead or not by putting a tick in the relevant column of the table below:

	Overhead?	
Cost	Yes	No
• Wages of staff paid on a piecework system.		✓
• Cost of factory canteen staff hourly wages.	✓	
• Direct materials.		✓

COST CARDS, TOTAL COSTS AND UNIT COSTS

45 JEEPERS LTD

Indicate whether the following costs are direct or not by putting a tick in the relevant column of the table below:

Cost	Yes	No
• Materials used in production.	✓	
• Piecework labour costs.	✓	
• Salary of chief executive.		✓

Jeepers Ltd makes a single product. At a production level of 15,000 units, the company has the following costs:

Materials   37,500 kilos at £14.00 per kilo

Labour   7,500 hours at £16.00 per hour

Overheads   £570,000

Complete the table below to show the unit product cost at the production level of 15,000 units. Give your answer to the nearest pound.

Element	Unit product cost
Materials	£ 35
Labour	£ 8
Direct cost	£ 43
Overheads	£ 38
Total	£ 81

46 BRANIAC LTD

Braniac Ltd makes a single product. A production level of 55,000 units has the following costs:

Materials   96,250 litres at £14 per litre

Labour   192,500 hours at £11.50 per hour

Overheads   £687,500

Complete the following unit cost table for a production level of 55,000 units. Give your answer to the nearest penny.

Element	Unit cost
Materials	£ 24.50
Labour	£ 40.25
Direct cost	£ 64.75
Overheads	£ 12.50
Total	£ 77.25

47 GLORIA LTD

Gloria Ltd is costing a single product which has the following cost details:

Variable costs per unit

Materials   £2

Labour   £3

Royalties   £0.50

Total fixed costs

Production overhead   £80,000

Sales and distribution   £90,000

Complete the following total cost and unit cost table for a production level of 20,000 units. Give your answer to the nearest penny for the unit cost and the nearest pound for the total cost.

Element	Unit cost		Total cost for 20,000 units	
Variable production costs	£	5,50	£	110 000
Fixed production costs	£	4,00	£	80 000
Total production cost	£	9,50	£	190 000

48 BIZARRO LTD

Bizarro Ltd makes a single product and for a production level of 17,000 units has the following cost details:

	Per unit	Cost
Materials	2.5kg	£18/kilo
Labour	1.0hrs	£9/hour
Fixed overheads		£42,500

Complete the table below to show the unit cost and total cost at the production level of 17,000 units. Give your answer to the nearest penny for the unit cost and the nearest pound for total cost.

Element	Unit cost		Total cost	
Materials	£	45	£	765 000
Labour	£	9	£	153 000
Overheads	£	2,50	£	42 500
Total	£	56,50	£	960 500

49 VINNY LTD

Vinny Ltd is a commercial laundrette below are the costings for 15,000 units:

Variable costs

Materials	£75,000	– 5
Labour	£120,000	– 8

Fixed costs

Production overhead	£100,000	– 6,67

Complete the following total cost and unit cost table for a REVISED production level of 20,000 units. Give your answer to the nearest penny for the unit cost and the nearest pound for total cost.

Element	Unit cost		Total cost	
Materials	£	5	£	100 000
Labour	£	8	£	160 000
Overheads	£	5.	£	100 000
Total	£	18	£	360 000

50   DARKSEID LTD

Darkseid Ltd makes a single product and for a production level of 95,000 units has the following cost details:

Materials	47,500kg	at £7/kilo
Labour	71,250hrs	at £9/hour
Fixed overheads		£242,000

Complete the table below to show the unit cost at a REVISED production level of 100,000 units. Give your answer to the nearest penny.

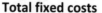

Element	Unit cost	
Materials	£	3,5
Labour	£	6,75
Fixed overheads	£	2,42
Total	£	12,67

(handwritten to the right of Materials row: 3,5)

51   DOOMSDAY LTD

Doomsday Ltd is costing a single product which has the following cost details:

Variable costs per unit	*Per unit*	*Cost*
Materials	45kg	£0.50/kg
Labour	2.5hrs	£16/hour

Total fixed costs	
Production overhead	£75,000
Administration overhead	£110,000
Sales and distribution	£75,000

Complete the following total cost and unit cost table for a production level of 20,000 units. Give your answer to the nearest penny for the unit cost and the nearest pound for total cost.

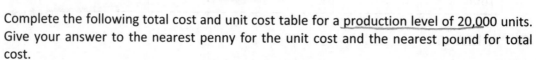

Element	Total cost for 20,000 units	Unit cost
Direct costs	£ 1250000	£ 62,50
Production overhead	£ 75 000	£ 3,75
Non production overhead	£ 185 000	£ 9,25
Total costs	£ 1 510 000	£ 75,50

52   OLSEN LTD

Olsen Ltd is costing a single product which has the following cost details:

Variable costs	*Per unit*
Materials	£12
Labour	£17
Total Fixed Costs	
Production overhead	£80,000
Administration overhead	£40,000

Complete the following total cost and unit cost table for a production level of 80,000 units. Give your answer to the nearest penny for the unit cost and the nearest pound for total cost.

Element	Total cost	Unit cost
Materials	£ 960 000	£ 12
Labour	£ 1 360 000	£ 17
Production overheads	£ 80 000	£ 1
Administration overheads	£ 40 000	£ 0,5
Total	£ 2 440 000	£ 30,50

53 FLAKEWAY LTD

Flakeway Ltd makes a single product and for a production level of 24,000 units has the following cost details:

Materials	6,000kg	at £20/kilo
Labour	8,000hrs	at £12/hour
Fixed overheads		£48,000

Complete the table below to show the unit cost at the production level of 24,000 units. Give your answer to the nearest penny.

Element	Unit cost
Materials	£ 5
Labour	£ 4
Fixed overheads	£ 2
Total	£ 11

54 CORONATION LTD

Coronation Ltd is costing a single product which has the following cost details

Variable costs	Per unit	Cost
Materials	50g =0,05	£10/kg = 0,5
Labour	1hr	£6/hour = 6
Total fixed costs		
Production overhead	£40,000	
Administration overhead	£20,000	
Sales and distribution	£25,000	

Complete the following total cost and unit cost table for a production level of 5,000 units. Give your answer to the nearest penny for the unit cost and the nearest pound for total cost.

Element	Total cost for 5,000 units	Unit cost
Direct costs	£ 32 500	£ 6,50
Production overhead	£ 40 000	£ 8
Non production overhead	£ 45 000	£ 9
Total costs	£ 117 500	£ 23,50

55 LUTHOR LTD

Luthor Ltd makes a single product and for a production level of 15,000 units has the following cost details:

Materials	60,000kg	at £15/ kilo
Labour	37,500hrs	at £9/hour
Fixed overheads		£570,000

Complete the table below to show the unit cost at the production level of 15,000 units. Give your answer to the nearest penny.

Element	Unit cost
Materials	£ 60
Labour	£ 22,50
Fixed overheads	£ 38
Total	£ 120,50

MANUFACTURING ACCOUNTS

56 JOKER LTD

Reorder the following costs into a manufacturing account format on the right side of the table below for the year ended 31 December.

	£		£	
Closing inventory of work in progress	52,000	Op. inv raw m	50 000	✓
Direct labour	140,000	Purch. raw m	120 000	✓
Opening inventory of raw materials	50,000	Closing inv. raw	65000	✓
Closing inventory of finished goods	61,000	Direct mat. usd	105000	✓
Closing inventory of raw materials	65,000	Direct labour	140 000	✓
Manufacturing overheads	85,000	Direct cost	245 000	
COST OF GOODS SOLD	322,000	Man. overh	185 000	✓
MANUFACTURING COST	330,000	Man. cost	330 000	✓
Purchases of raw materials	120,000	Op. inv WIP	48000	✓
Opening inventory of work in progress	48,000	Clos. WIP	52 000	✓
Opening inventory of finished goods	57,000	Cost manuf.	326 000	
DIRECT COST	245,000	Op. fin g.	57000	✓
DIRECT MATERIALS USED	105,000	Cl. fin g.	61000	✓
COST OF GOODS MANUFACTURED	326,000	Cost of goods sd	322000	✓

Enter the correct figures for the following costs which were not provided in the table above.

	£
DIRECT MATERIALS USED	105000
DIRECT COST	245000
MANUFACTURING COST	330 000
COST OF GOODS MANUFACTURED	326000
COST OF GOODS SOLD	322000

57   TUT LTD

Reorder the following costs into a manufacturing account format on the right side of the table below for the year ended 31 July.

	£		£
COST OF GOODS MANUFACTURED			
Opening inventory of work in progress	12,000	Op. raw mat. 10 000	
Opening inventory of raw materials	10,000	Purch. raw mat 60 000	
COST OF GOODS SOLD		Clos. raw mat 12000	
Closing inventory of finished goods	20,000	Direct mat. used 58 000	
Closing inventory of raw materials	12,000	Direct labour 88000	
Manufacturing overheads	45,000	Direct cost 146000	
MANUFACTURING COST		Manuf. overh. 45000	
Purchases of raw materials	60,000	Manuf. cost 191000	
Opening inventory of finished goods	18,000	Op. WiP 12000	
DIRECT COST		Closing WiP 15000	
Direct labour	88,000	Cost of manuf. 188000	
Closing inventory of work in progress	15,000	Op. Finish g. 18000	
DIRECT MATERIALS USED		Cl. fin. goods 20000	
		Goods sold 186000	

Enter the correct figures for the following costs which were not provided in the table above.

	£
DIRECT MATERIALS USED	58000
DIRECT COST	146000
MANUFACTURING COST	191 000
COST OF GOODS MANUFACTURED	188 000
COST OF GOODS SOLD	186000

58   RIDDLER LTD

Reorder the following costs into a manufacturing account format on the right side of the table below for the year ended 31 May. Enter the correct figures for the costs in bold that are not provided.

	£		£
DIRECT COST		Open raw mat	14000
Closing inventory of raw materials	20,000	Purch. r.m	100000
Closing inventory of work in progress	20,000	Clos. raw mat	20000
Opening inventory of finished goods	60,000	Direct mat.	94000
Direct labour	194,000	Direct lab.	194000
Closing inventory of finished goods	50,000	Direct cost	288000
Manufacturing overheads	106,000	Manuf. overh.	106000
Purchases of raw materials	100,000	Manuf. cost	394000
Opening inventory of work in progress	16,000	Open. WIP	16000
COST OF GOODS SOLD		Clos. WIP	20000
DIRECT MATERIALS USED		Cost manuf.	390000
Opening inventory of raw materials	14,000	Open. finished	60000
MANUFACTURING COST		Clos. finished	50000
COST OF GOODS MANUFACTURED		Cost goods sold	400000

59   CLOCKING LTD

Reorder the following costs into a manufacturing account format on the right side of the table below for the year ended 31 May. Enter the correct figures for the costs in bold that are not provided.

	£		£
Closing inventory of work in progress	10,000	Op. raw mat	7000
Direct labour	97,000	Purch. raw mat	50000
Opening inventory of raw materials	7,000	Clos. raw mat.	10000
Closing inventory of finished goods	25,000	Direct mater.	47000
Closing inventory of raw materials	10,000	Direct labour	97000
Manufacturing overheads	53,000	Direct cost	144000
COST OF GOODS SOLD		Manuf. overh.	53000
MANUFACTURING COST		Manuf. cost	197000
Purchases of raw materials	50,000	Open. WIP	8000
Opening inventory of work in progress	8,000	Clos. WIP	10000
Opening inventory of finished goods	30,000	Cost manuf.	195000
DIRECT COST		Open. finished	30000
DIRECT MATERIALS USED		Closing finish	25000
COST OF GOODS MANUFACTURED		Cost sold	200000

60 BOOKWORM LTD

Reorder the following costs into a manufacturing account format on the right side of the table below for the year ended 31 December. Enter the correct figures for the costs in bold that are not provided.

	£		£	
DIRECT COST ✓		Open. raw	5000	✓
Direct labour ✓	15,000	Purch. raw	15000	✓
MANUFACTURING COST ✓		Closing raw	(8000)	U
Opening inventory of raw materials ✓	5,000	Direct mat.	12000	✓
Closing inventory of finished goods ✓	16,000	Direct lab.	15000	✓
Purchases of raw materials ✓	15,000	Direct cost	27000	✓
DIRECT MATERIALS USED ✓		Manuf. overh.	25000	U
Manufacturing overheads ✓	25,000	Manuf. cost	52000	✓
Closing inventory of raw materials ✓	8,000	Open. WIP	4000	✓
COST OF GOODS SOLD		Clos. WIP	(6000)	✓
COST OF GOODS MANUFACTURED ✓		Cost of goods man.	50000	✓
Opening inventory of finished goods ✓	12,000	Open. finish	12000	✓
Opening inventory of work in progress ✓	4,000	Clos. finish	(16000)	✓
Closing inventory of work in progress ✓	6,000	Cost goods sold	46000	✓

61 MULTI

Within a manufacturing account, the manufacturing costs are £45,000. Opening work in progress is £11,000, while opening finished goods were costed at £8,100. Closing work in progress is £9,700, while closing finished goods were £8,900.

What is Multi's cost of goods sold?

- A £44,500
- B £48,700
- C £45,500
- D £41,300

Manuf. costs – 45000
Open. WIP – 11000
Closing WIP 9700
Open. finished – 8100
closing finished 8900

COSTING FOR INVENTORY AND WORK-IN-PROGRESS

NARRATIVE STYLE QUESTIONS

62 BOBBLE LTD

Match the disadvantage to the method of stock valuation by placing a tick in the relevant column of the table below:

Characteristic	FIFO	LIFO	AVCO
• Potentially out of date valuation on issues.	✓		
• The valuation of inventory rarely reflects the actual purchase price of the material.			✓
• Potentially out of date closing inventory valuation.		✓	

63 LINT LTD

Identify the following statements as either true or false by putting a tick in the relevant column of the table below:

Statement	True	False
• In periods of rising prices, FIFO gives a higher valuation of closing inventory than LIFO or AVCO.	✓	
• In periods of falling prices, LIFO gives a higher valuation of issues of inventory than FIFO or AVCO.		✓
• AVCO would normally be expected to produce a valuation of closing inventory somewhere between valuations under FIFO and LIFO.	✓	

64 FLUFF LTD

Identify the correct inventory valuation method from the characteristic given by putting a tick in the relevant column of the table below:

Characteristic	FIFO	LIFO	AVCO
• This inventory valuation method is particularly suited to inventory that consist of liquid materials e.g. oil.			✓
• This inventory valuation method is particularly suited to inventory that has a short shelf life e.g. dairy products.	✓		
• This inventory valuation method is suited to a wheat farmer who has large silos of grain. Grain is added to and taken from the top of these silos.		✓	

65 FIDO LTD

Identify the correct inventory valuation method from the characteristic given by putting a tick in the relevant column of the table below:

Characteristic	FIFO	LIFO	AVCO
• In times of rising prices this method will give higher profits.	✓		
• In times of rising prices this method will give lower profits.		✓	
• In times of rising prices this method gives a middle level of profits compared to the other two.			✓

66 TRUFFEAUX LTD

Identify whether the following statements are true or false by putting a tick in the relevant column of the table below:

Statement	True	False
• FIFO costs issues of inventory at the most recent purchase price.		✓
• AVCO costs issues of inventory at the oldest purchase price.		✓
• LIFO costs issues of inventory at the oldest purchase price.	✓	
• FIFO values closing inventory at the most recent purchase price.	✓	
• LIFO values closing inventory at the most recent purchase price.		✓
• AVCO values closing inventory at the latest purchase price.		✓

67 STOCKY LTD

Identify the correct inventory valuation method from the characteristic given by putting a tick in the relevant column of the table below:

Characteristic	FIFO	LIFO	AVCO
• Issues are valued at the most recent purchase cost.		✓	
• Inventory is valued at the average of the cost of purchases.			✓
• Inventory is valued at the most recent purchase cost.	✓		

IDENTIFICATION OF INVENTORY VALUATION METHOD

68   EPIC LTD

You are told that the opening inventory of a single raw material in the stores is 8,000 units at £5 per unit. During the month, 12,000 units at £4.50 were received and the following week 14,000 units were issued.

Task 1

Identify the valuation method described in the statements below:

Characteristic	FIFO	LIFO	AVCO
• Closing inventory is valued at £28,200.			✓
• The issue of inventory is valued at £67,000.	✓		
• The issue of inventory is valued at £64,000.		✓	

Task 2

Identify whether the statements in the table below are true or false by putting a tick in the relevant column.

	True	False
• AVCO values the issue of inventory at £65,800.	✓	
• LIFO values the closing inventory at £27,000.		✓
• FIFO values the closing inventory at £30,000.		✓

69   AWESOME LTD

You are told that the opening inventory of a single raw material in the stores is 6,000 units at £6 per unit. During the month, another 6,000 units at £10 were received and the following week 7,150 units were issued.

Task 1

Identify the valuation method described in the statements below:

Characteristic	FIFO	LIFO	AVCO
• Closing inventory is valued at £48,500.	✓		
• The issue of inventory is valued at £57,200.			✓
• The issue of inventory is valued at £66,900.		✓	

Task 2

Identify whether the statements in the table below are true or false by putting a tick in the relevant column.

	True	False
• FIFO values the issue of inventory at £47,500.	✓	
• AVCO values the closing inventory at £38,400.		✓
• LIFO values the closing inventory at £29,100.	✓	

70   AMAZING LTD

You are told that the opening inventory of a single raw material in the stores is 2,000 units at £1.50 per unit. During the month, another 5,000 units at £5 were received and the following week 6,000 units were issued.

Task 1

Identify the valuation method described in the statements below:

Characteristic	FIFO	LIFO	AVCO
• Closing inventory is valued at £1,500.		✔	
• The issue of inventory is valued at £23,000.	✔		
• The issue of inventory is valued at £24,000.			✔

Task 2

Identify whether the statements in the table below are true or false by putting a tick in the relevant column.

	True	False
• LIFO values the issue of inventory at £26,500.	✔	
• AVCO values the closing inventory at £5,000.		✔
• LIFO values the closing inventory at £4,000.		✔

INVENTORY CARDS

71   STONE LTD

Stone Ltd sells stone to builders. It had the following movements in one type of stone for the month of June.

DATE	RECEIPTS		ISSUES	
	Tonnes	Cost	Tonnes	Cost
June 1	500	£7,500		
June 8	350	£6,125		
June 15	275	£4,950		
June 22			650 ✓	
June 29	500	£8,750		

Complete the table below for the issue and closing inventory values, stating your answers to the nearest pound.

Method	Cost of issue on 22 June	Closing inventory at 30 June
FIFO	£ 10125	£ 17200
LIFO	£ 11450	£ 15875
AVCO	£ 10731	£ 16594

72 NATAL LTD

Natal Ltd makes and sells a wide range of clothes for babies. The following is an inventory card for Natal's most popular product for the month of December.

DATE	RECEIPTS		ISSUES	
	Units	Cost	Units	Cost
December 3	10,000	£85,000		
December 18	14,000	£112,000		
December 19	50,000	£350,000		
December 25			72,500	
December 29	5,000	£30,000		

Task 1

Complete the table below for the issue and closing inventory values. Give your answers to the nearest pound.

Method	Cost of issue on 25 Dec	Closing inventory at 29 Dec
LIFO	£ 534250	£ 42750
AVCO	£ 535775	£ 41225

Task 2

Identify the following statements as true or false by putting a tick in the relevant column of the table below:

	True	False
• FIFO would give a lower closing inventory valuation on the 29 December than LIFO and AVCO.	✓	
• FIFO would give a lower cost of issue on the 25 December than LIFO and AVCO.		✓

73 GANDALF LTD

Gandalf Ltd has the following movements in a certain type of inventory into and out of its stores for the month of July.

DATE	RECEIPTS			ISSUES			BALANCE
	Units	Unit cost	Total £	Units	Unit cost	Total £	Total £
July 2	600	£1.50	£900				
July 4	500	£1.70	£850				
July 15				620			
July 19	200	£1.80	£360				
July 31				400			

Calculate the costs of the issues made on July 15 and July 31 if Gandalf plc uses a LIFO inventory valuation method.

	Valuation £
• July 15	*1030*
• July 31	*660* ?

74 GRUNDY LTD

Grundy Ltd has the following movements in a certain type of inventory into and out of its stores for the month of October.

DATE	RECEIPTS		ISSUES	
	Units	Cost	Units	Cost
October 9	6000	£15,000		
October 12	3000	£6,000 *1000*		
October 20	3000	£3,000		
October 25			8500	
October 30	1000	£1,500		

Complete the table below for the issue and closing inventory values.

Method	Cost of issue on 25 October	Closing inventory at 31 October
FIFO	£ *20000*	£ *5500*
LIFO	£ *15250*	£
AVCO	£	£

75 LOBO LTD

Lobo Ltd has the following movements in a certain type of inventory into and out of its stores for the month of May.

DATE	RECEIPTS		ISSUES	
	Units	Cost	Units	Cost
May 12	250	£1,375		
May 17	400	£1,800		
May 18	600	£1,200		
May 29			500	
May 30	100	£375		

Complete the table below for the issue and closing inventory values.

Method	Cost of issue on 29 May	Closing inventory at 30 May
FIFO	£ *2500*	£ *2250*
LIFO	£ *1000*	£ *3750*
AVCO	£ *1750*	£ *3000*

76 ZOD LTD

Zod Ltd has the following movements in a certain type of inventory into and out of it stores for the month of February.

DATE	RECEIPTS		ISSUES	
	Units	Cost	Units	Cost
February 2	100 *50*	£500 *250*		
February 3			50	*250*
February 12	150 *140*	£600 *336*		
February 16	*120*	*392*	60	*255* *268*
February 20	110	£505		
February 26			40	*136*

Complete the table below for the issue and closing inventory values. State your answer to the nearest pound.

Method	Cost of issue on 16 February	Closing inventory at 26 February
FIFO	£ *290* ✓	£ *905* ✓
AVCO	£ *255* ✓	£ *964* ?

COSTING FOR LABOUR

NARRATIVE STYLE QUESTIONS

77 NULAB LTD

Identify the labour payment method by putting a tick in the relevant column of the table below:

Payment method	Time-rate	Piecework	Piece-rate plus bonus
• Labour is paid based solely on the production achieved.		✓	
• Labour is paid extra if an agreed level of output is exceeded.			✓
• Labour is paid according to hours worked.	✓		

78   LU LTD

Identify one advantage for each labour payment method by putting a tick in the relevant column of the table below:

Payment method	Time-rate	Piecework	Time-rate plus bonus
• Assured level of remuneration for employee.	✓		
• Employee earns more if they work more efficiently than expected.		✓	
• Assured level of remuneration and reward for working efficiently.			✓

79   MANDELA LTD

Identify whether the following statements are true or false in the relevant column of the table below:

Statement	True	False
• Time rate is paid based on the production achieved.		✓
• Overtime is paid for hours worked over the standard hours agreed.	✓	
• Piece rate is paid according to hours worked.		✓

80   PERRES LTD

Identify the hourly payment method by putting a tick in the relevant column of the table below:

Payment method	Basic rate	Overtime premium	Overtime rate
• This is the amount paid above the basic rate for hours worked in excess of the normal hours.		✓	✗
• This is the total amount paid per hour for hours worked in excess of the normal hours.		✗	✓
• This is the amount paid per hour for normal hours worked.	✓		

81   TEVEZ LTD

Identify the following statements as true or false by putting a tick in the relevant column of the table below:

Statement	True	False
• Direct labour costs can be identified with the goods being made or the service being provided.	✓	
• Indirect labour costs vary directly with the level of activity.		✓

82   BERDYCH LTD

Identify the whether the labour payment is usually associated with a fixed or variable cost by putting a tick in the relevant column of the table below:

Payment method	Variable	Fixed
• Labour that is paid based on a time rate basis per hour worked.	✓	
• Labour is paid on a monthly salary basis.		✓
• Labour that is based on number of units produced.	✓	

83   SODERLING LTD

Identify each labour payment method by putting a tick in the relevant column of the table below:

Payment method	Time-rate	Piecework	Salary
• Assured level of remuneration for employee usually agreed for the year.			✓
• Employee earnings are directly linked with units they produce.		✓	
• Employee earnings are directly linked with hours they work.	✓		

84   MURRAY LTD

Identify the following statements as true or false by putting a tick in the relevant column of the table below:

	True	False
• Indirect labour costs includes production supervisors' salaries.	✓	
• Direct labour costs usually vary directly with the level of activity.	✓	

85 OWEN LTD

Identify one advantage for each labour payment method by putting a tick in the relevant column of the table below:

Payment method	Time-rate	Piecework	Salary
• Employee is paid the same amount every month.			✓
• Employee wage increases in direct correlation with the number of hours worked.	✓		
• Employee wage increases in direct correlation with the number of units produced.		✓	

86 PIECEWORK STATEMENTS

Identify the following statements as either true or false by putting a tick in the relevant column of the table below:

Statement	True	False
• Piecework encourages employees to work harder.	✓	
• Piecework requires accurate recording of the number of hours staff have worked.		✓
• Piecework encourages workers to improve the quality of the units they produce.		✓

CALCULATING LABOUR COSTS

87 MUTANT LTD

Mutant Ltd pays a time-rate of £7.50 per hour to its direct labour for a standard 32 hour week. Any of the labour force working in excess of 32 hours is paid an overtime rate of time and a half.

Calculate the following figures for the week for the two workers in the table below, entering your answers to the nearest pound.

Worker	Hours worked	Basic wage	Overtime	Gross wage
S. Torm	34 hours	£ 240	£ 23	£ 263
J. Grey	38 hours	£ 240	£ 68	£ 308

88 PHOENIX LTD

Phoenix plc pays its employees £8.00 per hour and expects them to make 20 units per hour. Any excess production will be paid a bonus of £1.50 per unit.

Identify the following statements as being true or false by putting a tick in the relevant column of the table below:

Statement	True	False
An employee who works 38 hours and makes 775 units will not receive a bonus.		✓
An employee who works 40 hours and makes 815 units will receive total pay of £342.50.	✓	
An employee who works 37 hours and makes 744 units will earn a bonus of £6.	✓	

89 KAHN LTD

Kahn Ltd uses a time-rate method with bonus to pay its direct labour in one of its factories. The time-rate used is £12 per hour and a worker is expected to produce 5 units an hour, any time saved is paid at £6 per hour.

Calculate the gross wage for the week including bonus for the three workers in the table below:

Worker	Hours worked	Units produced	Basic wage	Bonus	Gross wage
A. Smith	35	175	£ 420	£ 0	£ 420
J. O'Hara	35	180	£ 420	£ 6	£ 426
M.Stizgt	35	185	£ 420	£ 12	£ 432

90 ENTERPRISE LTD

Enterprise Ltd pays a time-rate of £12 per hour to its direct labour force for a standard 35 hour week. Any of the labour force working in excess of 35 hours is paid an overtime rate of time and a half.

Calculate the gross wage for the week for the three workers in the table below:

Worker	Hours worked	Basic wage	Overtime	Gross wage
J. Picard	37 hours	£ 420	£ 36	£ 456
B. Crusher	42 hours	£ 420	£ 126	£ 546
D. Troi	31 hours	£ 372	£ 0	£ 372

91 SGC LTD

SGC Ltd uses a basic salary plus piecework method to pay labour in one of its factories. The basic salary is £285 per week the piece rate used is £0.75 per unit produced.

Calculate the gross wage for the week for the two workers in the table below. Enter your answer to the nearest penny.

Worker	Units produced in week	Gross wage
J. O'Neill	500 units	£ *660*
S. Carter	650 units	£ *772,50*

92 GOTHIC LTD

Gothic Ltd uses a time-rate method with bonus to pay its direct labour in one of its factories. The time-rate used is £17 per hour and a worker is expected to produce 8 units an hour, anything over this and the worker is paid a bonus of £5 per unit.

Calculate the gross wage for the week including bonus for the three workers in the table below:

Worker	Hours worked	Units produced	Basic wage	Bonus	Gross wage
M. Shelley	37	300	£ *629*	£ *20*	£ *649*
G. Leroux	37	312	£ *629*	£ *80*	£ *709*
E. A. Poe	37	296	£ *629*	£ *0*	£ *629*

296

93 AVENGERS LTD

Avengers Ltd pays a time-rate of £10 per hour to its direct labour force a standard 35 hour week. Any of the labour force working in excess of this over the four week period is paid an overtime rate of time and a quarter. *12,50*

Calculate the gross wage for the **4-week** period for the three workers in the table below. Enter your answers to the nearest pound.

Worker	Hours worked	Basic wage	Overtime	Gross wage
T. Stark	138	£ *1380*	£ *0*	£ *1380*
B. Banner	142	£ *1400*	£ *25*	£ *1425*
S. Rogers	145	£ *1400*	£ *63*	£ *1463*

94   DRACO LTD

Draco Ltd uses a piecework method to pay labour in one of its factories. The rate used is 80p per unit produced up to the standard number of units to be produced per week of 250. For any units over that the workers will get £10 per 20 units.

Calculate the gross wage for the week for the three workers in the table below:

Worker	Units produced in week	Gross wage
P. Jones	240 units	£ 192
D. Bannatyne	350 units	£ 200 + 50 = 250
L. Redford	250 units	£ 200

95   QUAGGA PLC

Quagga plc pays its employees £4.50 per hour and expects them to make 50 units per hour. Any excess production will be paid a bonus of 45p per unit.

Identify the following statements as being true or false by putting a tick in the relevant column of the table below:

Statement	True	False
During a 29 hour week, an employee producing 1,475 units would not receive a bonus.		✓
During a 32 hour week, an employee producing 1,665 units would receive a bonus of £29.25.	✓	
During a 37 hour week, an employee producing 1,925 units would receive total pay of £300.25.		✓

96   JLA PLC

JLA plc pays its employees £5 per hour and expects them to make 6 units per hour. Any time saved will be paid as a bonus at £8 per hour.

Identify the following statements as being true or false by putting a tick in the relevant column of the table below:

Statement	True	False
During a 30 hour week, an employee producing 192 units would receive a bonus of £16.	✓	
During a 35 hour week, an employee producing 240 units would receive total pay of £215.	✓	
During a 30 hour week, an employee producing 180 units would not receive a bonus.	✓	

97   INJUSTICE LTD

Davidson Ltd pays a basic wage of £175/week plus £1.20 per unit produced.

Calculate the gross wage for the week for the three workers in the table below:

Worker	Units produced	Basic wage	Piece work	Gross wage
N. Wing	295	£ 175	£ 354	£ 529
W. Woman	355	£ 175	£ 426	£ 601
T. Flash	385	£ 175	£ 462	£ 637

98   GREENWOOD LTD

Greenwood Ltd pays a basic wage of £350/week equivalent to a time-rate of £10 per hour and a standard 35 hour week. Workers are expected to produce 5 units an hour and for units produced in excess of this a bonus is paid based on £7 for every hour saved.

So, for example, if 10 additional units are produced, then this would be equivalent to two hours saved and a bonus of £14 awarded.

Calculate the gross wage for the week including bonus for the three workers in the table below:

Worker	Hours worked	Units produced	Basic wage	Bonus	Gross wage
B. Ryan	35	175	£ 350	£ 0	£ 350
S. Chang	35	190	£ 350	£ 21	£ 371
E. Schneider	35	210	£ 350	£ 49	£ 399

SPREADSHEETS AND VARIANCES

NARRATIVE QUESTIONS

99   VARIOUS LTD

Identify the following statements as being true or false by putting a tick in the relevant column of the table below:

Statement	True	False
• A variance is the difference between budgeted and actual cost.	✓	
• A favourable variance means actual costs are less than budgeted.	✓	
• An adverse variance means that actual income is less than budgeted.	✓	✓
• A spreadsheet can be used to store large amounts of financial information.	✓	

100 SPREADSHEETS

Identify the following statements about spreadsheets as being true or false by putting a tick in the relevant column of the table below:

Statement	True	False
• Cells are used to enter data into a spreadsheet.	✓	
• Spreadsheets cannot be protected, meaning that the data they contain is open for anyone to see.		✓
• The 'worksheet' refers to the entire spreadsheet file.		✓
• The 'sum' function is the only formula that can be used to sum a number of figures in a spreadsheet.		✓

101 STUFF LTD

Identify the following statements about spreadsheets as being true or false by putting a tick in the relevant column of the table below:

Statement	True	False
• Information can be entered into a spreadsheet either through typing it into the active cell or by entering it into the formula bar.	✓	
• All formulas have to start with an equals sign (=) to be recognized by the spreadsheet.	✓	
• Spreadsheet functions are only designed to allow users to add, subtract, multiply and divide figures.		✓
• Spreadsheets will not allow the user to display the information they contain using graphs.		✓

VARIANCE SPREADSHEET QUESTIONS

102 EREBOR PLC

Erebor Ltd has produced a spreadsheet detailing budgeted and actual cost for last month.

Task 1

Calculate the amount of the variance for each cost type and then determine whether it is adverse or favourable (enter A or F).

	A	B	C	D	E
1	Cost type	Budget £	Actual £	Variance £	Adverse or favourable (A or F)
2	Sales	600,500	597,800	2700	A
3	Direct materials	205,800	208,500	2700	A
4	Direct labour	155,000	154,800	200	F
5	Production overheads	65,000	72,100	7100	A
6	Administration overheads	58,400	55,200	3200	F

Task 2

Insert the formulas in the table below that you used for cells 2 to 6 of column D.

	D
1	Variance
2	=Sum(B2+C2) =
3	
4	
5	
6	

Task 3

In a typical spreadsheet programme, which of the following function buttons could be used to put the variance figures in cells D2 to D6 in ascending order?

Select ONE of A, B, C or D.

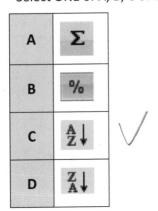

A	Σ
B	%
C	A↓Z↓
D	Z↓A↓

103 MORIA LTD

The following spreadsheet for this month has been produced for Moria Ltd. Any variance in excess of 7% of budget is deemed to be significant.

Task 1

Calculate the variance as a % of the budget and enter your answer into the table below to the **nearest whole percentage**. Indicate whether the variance is significant or not by entering S for significant and NS for not significant.

	A	B	C	D	E
1	Cost type	Budget	Variance	Variance as % of budget	Significant or Not significant
2	Sales	45,100	4,214	9%	S
3	Material	15,750	1,260	8%	S
4	Labour	12,915	805	6%	NS
5	Variable overheads	5,750	315	5%	NS
6	Fixed overheads	8,155	1,011	12%	S

Task 2

Insert the formulas in the table below that you used for cells 2 to 6 of column D.

	D
1	Variance as % of budget
2	=C2/B2
3	
4	
5	
6	

104 WYEDALE LTD

Wyedale Ltd has produced a spreadsheet detailing budgeted and actual cost for last month.

Calculate the amount of the variance in £ and % for each cost type and then determine whether it is adverse or favourable by putting an A or F the relevant column of the table below. State your percentage to the nearest whole number.

	A	B	C	D	E	F
1	Cost type	Budget £	Actual £	Variance £	Variance %	Adverse/ Favourable
2	Sales	27,000	29,775	2775	10	F
3	Direct materials	7,400	8,510	1110	15	A
4	Direct labour	7,200	7,920	720	10	A
5	Production overheads	5,500	5,390	110	2	F
6	Administration overheads	4,500	4,365	135	3	F

105 BELEGOST LTD

The following spreadsheet for this month has been produced for Belegost Ltd as summarised in the table below. Any variance in excess of 6% of budget is deemed to be significant and should be reported to the relevant manager for review and appropriate action.

Task 1

Determine whether the variance for each figure is adverse or favourable by putting an A or F into the relevant column of the table below. Put an S in column E if the variance is significant or an NS if the variance is not significant.

	A	B	C	D	E
1		Budget £	Actual £	Adverse or Favourable (A or F)	Significant or not significant (S or NS)
2	Sales	205,000	207,100	F	NS
3	Direct materials	75,150	78,750	A	NS
4	Direct labour	110,556	107,950	F	NS
5	Production overheads	14,190	12,500	F	S
6	Non-production overheads	16,190	17,880	A	S

Task 2

Place the figures from column C into the following table in **descending** order.

	C
1	*Actual*
2	12500
3	1788
4	7841
5	10780
6	20710

106 IVAN LTD

Ivan Ltd has produced a spreadsheet detailing budgeted and actual cost for last month.

Task 1

Calculate the amount of the variance for each cost type and then determine whether it is adverse or favourable by putting an A or an F into the relevant column below:

	A	B	C	C	E
1	Cost type	Budget £	Actual £	Variance £	Significant or Not Significant (S or NS)
2	Sales	544,750	547,450	2700 F	NS
3	Direct materials	76,800	80,200	3400 A	NS
4	Direct labour	148,400	146,000	2400 F	NS
5	Production overheads	136,000	144,200	8200 A	S
6	Administration overheads	105,000	109,800	4800 A	NS

Task 2

Insert the formulas in the table below that you used for cells 2 to 6 of column D.

	D
1	*Variance* £
2	=C2-B2
3	
4	
5	
6	

107   BLUEBELL LTD

The following spreadsheet for this month has been produced for Bluebell Ltd as summarised in the table below.

Task 1

Calculate the variances in the spreadsheet below and indicate whether they are adverse or favourable by putting an A or F in the relevant column and calculate the variance as a % to the nearest whole number.

	A	B	C	D	E	F
1	Cost type	Budget £	Actual £	Variance £	Adverse/ Favourable	%
2	Sales	£204,555	£197,455	7100	A	3
3	Direct materials	£39,000	£42,300	3300	A	8
4	Direct labour	£75,000	£83,000	8000	A	11
5	Production overheads	£69,000	£64,800	4200	F	6
6	Administration overheads	£53,000	£58,900	5900	A	11

Task 2

Insert the formulas in the table below that you used for cells 2 to 6 of column F.

	F
1	Variance £
2	=D2/B2*100
3	
4	
5	
6	

SPREADSHEET FORMAT QUESTIONS

108 ELVES LTD

Elves Ltd has started the production of a spreadsheet that will enable it to calculate its profit for each month of the first four months of the year. There was no opening or closing inventories. The first month has been completed.

Units sold:	January – 14,000
	February – 16,000
	March – 12,000
	April – 14,500
Variable costs	£0.95 per unit
Sales	£1.50 per unit
Fixed costs	£7,500 per month

	A	B	C	D	E
1		Sales £	Fixed costs ?	Variable costs	Profit ?
2	January	21,000	7,500	13,300	200
3	February	24000	7500	15200	1300
4	March	18000	7500	11400	−900
5	April	21750	7500	13775	475
6	Total	84750	30000	53675	1075

Task 1

Decide which of the following headings should be entered into each of the cells C1, D1 and E1: Profit/loss, variable costs, fixed costs.

Cell	Heading
C1	Fixed
D1	Var.
E1	Profit

Task 2

Complete the table above by entering the correct figures into the above table for rows 3 to 6 inclusive. Insert any losses as negative numbers.

Task 3

Insert the formulas in the table below that you used for row 6 of columns B, C, D and E.

	A	B	C	D	E
6	Total	=Sum B2:B5			

109 HOBBIT PLC

Hobbit plc has started the production of a spreadsheet that will enable it to calculate its total labour cost for the four weeks of the last month. The first week has been completed.

Hours worked: Week 1 – 2,566

                        Week 2 – 3,876

                        Week 3 – 4,663

                        Week 4 – 3,445

Average hourly rate paid   £12 per hour

Hobbit pays staff a bonus of 10% of their total standard pay each week where hours worked are in excess of 3,800.

	A	B	C	D	E	F
1		Standard hours	Standard hourly rate paid £	Total standard pay	Bonus	Gross pay
2	Week 1	2,566	12	30,792	0	30,792
3	Week 2	3876	12	46512	4651,2	
4	Week 3	4663	12	55956	5595,6	
5	Week 4	3445	12	41340	4134	

Task 1

Complete the above table by entering the correct figures into the above table for rows 2 to 5 inclusive. Work to the nearest whole £.

Task 2

Insert the formulas in the table below that you used for column D, rows 2 to 5 inclusive.

	D
1	Total standard pay
2	=B2*C2
3	
4	
5	

110 SMAUG PLC

Smaug plc has started the production of a spreadsheet that will enable it to calculate its profits for the last three months. The first month has been completed.

Units:	August – 1,100
	September – 2,000
	October – 1,500
Materials	£20 per unit
Labour	£12 per unit
Fixed overheads	£5000 per month
Sales	£35 per unit

	A	B	C	D	E
1		*August*	*September*	*October*	*Total*
2	*Labour*	13,200	24000	18000	55200
3	Materials	22,000	40000	30000	92000
4	Fixed overheads	5,000	5000	5000	15000
5	*Total costs*	40,200	69000	53000	162200
6	*? Sales*	38,500	70000	52500	161000
7	Profit/(loss)	(1,700)	1000	(500)	(1200)

Task 1

Decide which of the following headings should be entered into each of the cells A2, A5 and A6: Sales, Total costs, Labour.

Cell	Heading
A2	
A5	
A6	

Task 2

Complete the table above by entering the correct figures into the above table for columns 3 to 6 inclusive. Insert any losses as negative numbers.

Task 3

Insert the formulas in the table below that you used for row 7 of columns B, C, D and E.

	A	B	C	D	E
7	Profit/(loss)	= B6 - B5			

Section 2

ANSWERS TO PRACTICE QUESTIONS

COST CLASSIFICATION

FINANCIAL AND MANAGEMENT ACCOUNTING

1   FAMA

Characteristic	Financial accounting	Management accounting
• Have to be produced annually.	✓	
• Analyses historic events to help produce forecasts.		✓
• Is always produced using accounting standards.	✓	
• Is produced on an ad hoc basis when required.		✓

2   FINANCIAL AND MANAGEMENT

Characteristic	Financial accounting	Management accounting
• Must be presented as specified by the Companies Act and accounting standards.	✓	
• Helps managers run the business on a day-to-day basis.		✓
• Used as the basis for the calculation of the organisation's tax charge.	✓	
• Can include anything that managers feel is useful for the business.		✓

3   MAFA

Characteristic	Management accounting	Financial accounting
• It is based on past events.		✓
• Its purpose is to provide information for managers.	✓	
• It is based on future events.	✓	
• It complies with company law and accounting rules.		✓

4   FEATURES

Feature	Financial accounting	Management accounting
• Analysis of profit by cost centre.		✓
• Statement of profit or loss using format as dictated by accounting standards and company law.	✓	
• Cash flow forecasts.		✓
• Cost per unit calculation.		✓

COST AND PROFIT CENTRES

5   JEREMY

	Cost centre	Profit centre
• Bakery	✓	
• Shop		✓
• Office	✓	

6   PRINT PLC

Department	Cost centre	Profit centre
• Binding		✓
• Shops		✓
• Marketing	✓	

7   HOOCH PLC

Department	Cost centre	Profit centre	Investment centre
• Hooch's manager has no responsibility for income or asset purchases and disposals.	✓		
• Hooch's manager is assessed on the profitability of their department, as well as how effectively they have controlled their assets.			✓
• Hooch's manager is responsible for income and expenditure of their department only.		✓	

CLASSIFYING COSTS BY ELEMENT (MATERIALS, LABOUR OR OVERHEADS)

8   VVV LTD

Cost	Materials	Labour	Overheads
• Paint used on the planes.	✓		
• Depreciation of the machines used in the factory.			✓
• Oil used on the machines in the factory.			✓
• Salary of worker assembling the planes.		✓	

9   TRIP LTD

Cost	Materials	Labour	Overheads
• Wages of the insurance clerks dealing with claims.		✓	
• Rent of the office.			✓
• Paper used to print off insurance policies.	✓		
• Salary of the office manager.		✓	

10   FRUWT LTD

Cost	Materials	Labour	Overheads
• Purchase of fruit for juicing.	✓		
• Electricity used by juicing machines.			✓
• Water added to the juice before sale.	✓		
• Wages of staff operating juicing machinery.		✓	

11 MARTIN

Cost	Materials	Labour	Overheads
• Stationery used in Martin's court cases.	✓		
• Wages of Martin's secretary.		✓	
• Water rates for Martin's office.			✓
• Cost of training courses taken by Martin.			✓

CLASSIFYING COSTS BY NATURE (DIRECT OR INDIRECT)

12 RUSSELL

Cost	Direct	Indirect
• Paper used in the newspapers.	✓	
• Wages of warehouse staff.		✓
• Heat and light for head office.		✓
• Ink used in printing the newspapers.	✓	

13 RUSSETT LTD

Cost	Direct	Indirect
• Glass used to make tablets.	✓	
• Insurance of factory.		✓
• Wages of workers assembling tablets.	✓	
• Cost of entertaining corporate clients.		✓

14 SCOTLAND LTD

Cost	Direct	Indirect
• Cleaners' wages.		✓
• Advertising expense.		✓
• Material used in production.	✓	
• Production manager's wages.		✓
• Machinist wages.	✓	

15 DIRECT OR INDIRECT

Cost	Direct	Indirect
• Chargeable hour for a lawyer.	✓	
• Machine hire for a building contractor in a long term contract.	✓	
• Electricity for a garden centre.		✓
• Audit fee for a restaurant.		✓

16   DIRECT COSTS

B

Direct costs are variable and are therefore usually assumed to be constant, regardless of the level of activity within the relevant range. Answer A is incorrect because it describes the behaviour of a fixed cost within the relevant range of activity. Answer C also describes a fixed cost, since the same total fixed cost would be shared over a varying number of units, resulting in a unit cost that varies with changes in activity levels. Answer D is incorrect because total variable costs are conventionally deemed to remain unaltered when activity levels remain constant.

CLASSIFYING COSTS BY FUNCTION (PRODUCTION, ADMINISTRATION OR SELLING AND DISTRIBUTION)

17   NOOGLE LTD

Cost	Production	Administration	Selling and distribution
• Purchases of plastic for ready meal containers.	✓		
• Depreciation of sales department's delivery lorries.			✓
• Insurance of office computers.		✓	
• Salaries of production workers.	✓		

18   HEAVING LTD

Cost	Production	Administration	Selling and distribution
• Paper used to print off sales invoices.		✓	
• Metal used to make weights and bars.	✓		
• Depreciation of sales person's vehicle.			✓
• Repairs to machine in factory.	✓		

19 KORMA PLC

Cost	Production	Administration	Selling and distribution	Finance
• Direct materials.	✓			
• Sales director's salary.			✓	
• Head office printer ink.		✓		
• Direct labour.	✓			
• Bank charges.				✓

20 JAMES

Cost	Production	Administration	Selling and distribution	Finance
• Salary of receptionist.		✓		
• Plastic used in false teeth.	✓			
• Stationery provided to all departments.		✓		
• Interest on James' bank overdraft.				✓
• Electricity for James' factory.	✓			

CLASSIFYING COSTS BY BEHAVIOUR (FIXED, VARIABLE OR SEMI-VARIABLE)

21 QUARK LTD

Cost	Fixed	Variable	Semi-variable
• Bar manager's salary.	✓		
• Alcohol used to make drinks.		✓	
• Rent of bar.	✓		
• Telephone costs, including standard line rental charge.			✓

22 MORN LTD

Cost	Fixed	Variable	Semi-variable
• Wood used in production.		✓	
• Advertising manager's salary.	✓		
• Electricity costs which include a standing charge.			✓
• Labour costs paid on a piecework basis.		✓	

23 STEPPED FIXED COST

A

A supervisor's wages are usually classified as a step cost because a supervisor may be responsible for supervising up to a specific number of workers. However, if output increases such that additional direct labour is required, then an extra supervisor will be required.

| 1 – 10 workers | 1 supervisor |
| 11 – 20 workers | 2 supervisors |

24 BRAETAK LTD

Cost	Fixed	Variable	Semi-variable
• Rent of an office building.	✓		
• Wages of production staff paid on an hourly basis.		✓	
• Wages of production staff paid by a piece rate method.		✓	
• Sales staff paid a basic wage plus commission for each unit sold.			✓

Note: the piece rate scheme does not mention a guaranteed minimum wage so the correct answer is variable.

25 ODO LTD

Cost	Fixed	Variable	Semi-variable
• Material used in the production process.		✓	
• Safety review fee for the year.	✓		
• Electricity costs which include a standing charge.			✓
• Labour paid on a per unit basis.		✓	

26 DEFINITIONS

Behaviour	Fixed	Variable	Semi-variable	Stepped cost
• This type of cost increases in direct proportion to the amount of units produced.		✓		
• This type of cost has a fixed and a variable element.			✓	
• This type of cost remains constant despite changes in output.	✓			
• This type of cost is fixed within a certain range of output.				✓

27 MATCH A GRAPH

(a)   Variable cost per unit – graph 1

(b)   Total fixed cost – graph 1

(c)   Stepped fixed costs – graph 3

(d)   Total variable cost – graph 2

(e)   Semi-variable cost – graph 4

COST CODING

28 BYTES LTD

Cost	Code
• Salary of trainee IT consultant.	• B100
• Planning costs to renew lease of the office.	• C200
• Wages of the office manager.	• B200
• Cleaning materials used by cleaner.	• A200

29 HERO LTD

Transaction	Code
• Cost of major advertising campaign.	• 760/340
• Oil for machine in factory.	• 225/115
• Silk used in manufacturing of costumes.	• 225/110
• Insurance of head office.	• 485/230
• Sale of women's costumes to a supermarket chain.	• 115/085
• Wages paid to delivery van drivers.	• 760/340

30 VILLAIN LTD

Transaction	Code
• Petrol used to run drilling machinery.	• 015/200
• Sale of silver to a jewellery manufacturer.	• 011/200
• Replacement of worn out drilling machinery parts.	• 015/200
• Depreciation of fleet of delivery lorries.	• 024/200
• Salary of finance director.	• 019/200
• Sale of gold to an electronics company.	• 011/100

31 NAYULZ LTD

Cost		Code
•	Income earned from salons in New York City, America.	RE228
•	Bank loans raised to open a new store in London.	IN100
•	Nail polish purchased for use in salon.	CO315
•	Heat and light for salon.	CO325
•	Nayulz funds invested in new project.	IN110

32 JUMPER LTD

Sale		Code
•	Sale of one jumper to Mrs S. Wooley.	KNI/315
•	Sale of protective trousers to a factory in London.	TRS/635
•	Sale of large coats to an office in Birmingham.	MCN/515
•	Sale of woolen jumpers to a shop in Halifax.	KNI/425
•	Sale of four coats to Mr A. West.	MCN/315
•	Sale of three hundred trousers to a shop in Manchester.	TRS/425

33 GREENFINGERS

Cost		Code
•	Purchase of seeds used to grow plants for resale.	CS880
•	External loans for investment in new greenhouses.	IN515
•	Wages of gardeners who maintain the plants to be sold.	CS890
•	Sales of food and drink.	RV795

COST BEHAVIOUR

CALCULATION QUESTIONS

34 HULK PLC

Statement		Fixed	Variable	Semi-variable
•	Costs are £37,500 when 7,500 units are made and £62,500 when 12,500 units are made.		✓	
•	Costs are £2 per unit when 7,500 units are made and £1.20 per unit when 12,500 units are made.	✓		
•	Costs are £50,000 when 7,500 units are made and £80,000 when 12,500 units are made.			✓

35 BANNER PLC

Statement	Fixed	Variable	Semi-variable
• Costs are £5,000 plus £45 per unit, regardless of the number of units made.			✓
• Costs are £5,000 when 300 units are made and £5,000 when 600 units are made.	✓		
• Costs are £35 per unit regardless of the number of units made.		✓	

36 NORTON PLC

Statement	Fixed	Variable	Semi-variable
• Costs are £50,000 in total regardless of the number of units made.	✓		
• Costs are £50,000 in total when 2,500 units are made and £80,000 when 4,000 units are made.		✓	
• Costs are £7 per unit when 1,000 units are made and £6 per unit when 2,000 units are made.			✓

Note: The third cost must be semi-variable as it cannot be fixed (it changes as the number of units changes) and it cannot be purely variable as the cost per unit changes at different levels of activity.

NARRATIVE STYLE QUESTIONS

37 BUNGLE LTD

Statement	True	False
• Total variable costs will decrease.		✓
• Total fixed costs will remain the same.	✓	
• The variable cost per unit will remain the same.	✓	
• The fixed cost per unit will increase.		✓

38   TF

Statement	True	False
• Variable costs change directly with changes in activity.	✓	
• Fixed costs change directly with changes in activity.		✓
• Stepped costs are fixed within a set range of output.	✓	

39   FIXED OR VARIABLE

Cost	Fixed	Variable
• Direct materials.		✓
• Power used in production machinery.		✓
• Training costs for new employees in production.	✓	
• Insurance for sales cars.	✓	
• Insurance machinery.	✓	
• Sales commission.		✓

40   FOV

Cost	Fixed	Variable
• Piecework wages paid to factory workers.		✓
• Salaries paid to company directors.	✓	
• Annual payment for cleaning of air conditioning units.	✓	

41   VOF

Cost	Fixed	Variable
• Annual salaries paid to factory managers.	✓	
• Hourly wages paid to factory workers.		✓
• Colour ink used to print magazines.		✓

42   STORM

	Overhead?	
Cost	Yes	No
• Labour cost of workers who assemble the product.		✓
• Insurance cost of factory where product is assembled.	✓	
• Heat and light for manufacturing machines.	✓	

43   ROGUE

		Overhead?	
Cost		Yes	No
• Labour cost of cleaning staff in a factory.		✓	
• Depreciation of delivery vans.		✓	
• Cost of materials used to build the product.			✓

44   GAMBIT

		Overhead?	
Cost		Yes	No
• Wages of staff paid on a piecework system.			✓
• Cost of factory canteen staff hourly wages.		✓	
• Direct materials.			✓

COST CARDS, TOTAL COSTS AND UNIT COSTS

45   JEEPERS LTD

Cost		Yes	No
• Materials used in production.		✓	
• Piecework labour costs.		✓	
• Salary of chief executive.			✓

Element	Unit product cost
Materials	£35
Labour	£8
Direct cost	£43
Overheads	£38
Total	£81

46   BRANIAC LTD

Element	Unit cost
Materials	£24.50
Labour	£40.25
Direct cost	£64.75
Overheads	£12.50
Total	£77.25

47   GLORIA LTD

Element	Unit cost	Total cost for 20,000 units
Variable production costs	£5.50	£110,000
Fixed production costs	£4.00	£80,000
Total production cost	£9.50	£190,000

48   BIZARRO LTD

Element	Unit cost	Total cost
Materials	£45.00	£765,000
Labour	£9.00	£153,000
Overheads	£2.50	£42,500
Total	£56.50	£960,500

49   VINNY LTD

Element	Unit cost	Total cost
Materials	£5.00	£100,000
Labour	£8.00	£160,000
Overheads	£5.00	£100,000
Total	£18.00	£360,000

50   DARKSEID LTD

Element	Unit cost
Materials	£3.50
Labour	£6.75
Fixed overheads	£2.42
Total	£12.67

51   DOOMSDAY LTD

Element	Total cost for 20,000 units	Unit cost
Direct costs	£1,250,000	£62.50
Production overhead	£75,000	£3.75
Non production overhead	£185,000	£9.25
Total costs	£1,510,000	£75.50

52   OLSEN LTD

Element	Total cost	Unit cost
Materials	£960,000	£12.00
Labour	£1,360,000	£17.00
Production overheads	£80,000	£1.00
Administration overheads	£40,000	£0.50
Total	£2,440,000	£30.50

53   FLAKEWAY LTD

Element	Unit cost
Materials	£5.00
Labour	£4.00
Fixed overheads	£2.00
Total	£11.00

54   CORONATION LTD

	Total cost for 5,000 units	Unit cost
Direct costs	£32,500	£6.50
Production overhead	£40,000	£8.00
Non production overhead	£45,000	£9.00
Total costs	£117,500	£23.50

55   LUTHOR LTD

Element	Unit cost
Materials	£60.00
Labour	£22.50
Fixed overheads	£38.00
Total	£120.50

MANUFACTURING ACCOUNTS

56 JOKER LTD

Manufacturing account – Y/E 31 December

	£
Opening inventory of raw materials	50,000
Purchases of raw materials	120,000
Closing inventory of raw materials	65,000
DIRECT MATERIALS USED	
Direct labour	140,000
DIRECT COST	
Manufacturing overheads	85,000
MANUFACTURING COST	
Opening inventory of work in progress	48,000
Closing inventory of work in progress	52,000
COST OF GOODS MANUFACTURED	
Opening inventory of finished goods	57,000
Closing inventory of finished goods	61,000
COST OF GOODS SOLD	

	£
DIRECT MATERIALS USED	105,000
DIRECT COST	245,000
MANUFACTURING COST	330,000
COST OF GOODS MANUFACTURED	326,000
COST OF GOODS SOLD	322,000

57 TUT LTD

Manufacturing account – Y/E 31 July

	£
Opening inventory of raw materials	10,000
Purchases of raw materials	60,000
Closing inventory of raw materials	12,000
DIRECT MATERIALS USED	58,000
Direct labour	88,000
DIRECT COST	146,000
Manufacturing overheads	45,000
MANUFACTURING COST	191,000
Opening inventory of work in progress	12,000
Closing inventory of work in progress	15,000
COST OF GOODS MANUFACTURED	188,000
Opening inventory of finished goods	18,000
Closing inventory of finished goods	20,000
COST OF GOODS SOLD	186,000

	£
DIRECT MATERIALS USED	58,000
DIRECT COST	146,000
MANUFACTURING COST	191,000
COST OF GOODS MANUFACTURED	188,000
COST OF GOODS SOLD	186,000

58 RIDDLER LTD

Manufacturing account – Y/E 31 May

	£
Opening inventory of raw materials	14,000
Purchases of raw materials	100,000
Closing inventory of raw materials	20,000
DIRECT MATERIALS USED	**94,000**
Direct labour	194,000
DIRECT COST	**288,000**
Manufacturing overheads	106,000
MANUFACTURING COST	**394,000**
Opening inventory of work in progress	16,000
Closing inventory of work in progress	20,000
COST OF GOODS MANUFACTURED	**390,000**
Opening inventory of finished goods	60,000
Closing inventory of finished goods	50,000
COST OF GOODS SOLD	**400,000**

59 CLOCKING LTD

Manufacturing account – Y/E 31 May

	£
Opening inventory of raw materials	7,000
Purchases of raw materials	50,000
Closing inventory of raw materials	10,000
DIRECT MATERIALS USED	**47,000**
Direct labour	97,000
DIRECT COST	**144,000**
Manufacturing overheads	53,000
MANUFACTURING COST	**197,000**
Opening inventory of work in progress	8,000
Closing of work in progress	10,000
COST OF GOODS MANUFACTURED	**195,000**
Opening inventory of finished goods	30,000
Closing inventory of finished goods	25,000
COST OF GOODS SOLD	**200,000**

60   BOOKWORM LTD

Manufacturing account – Y/E 31 December

	£
Opening inventory of raw materials	5,000
Purchases of raw materials	15,000
Closing inventory of raw materials	8,000
DIRECT MATERIALS USED	**12,000**
Direct labour	15,000
DIRECT COST	**27,000**
Manufacturing overheads	25,000
MANUFACTURING COST	**52,000**
Opening inventory of work in progress	4,000
Closing inventory of work in progress	(6,000)
COST OF GOODS MANUFACTURED	**50,000**
Opening inventory of finished goods	12,000
Closing inventory of finished goods	(16,000)
COST OF GOODS SOLD	**46,000**

61   MULTI

C – Manufacturing cost + opening WIP – closing WIP + opening FG – closing FG

COSTING FOR INVENTORY AND WORK-IN-PROGRESS

NARRATIVE STYLE QUESTIONS

62   BOBBLE LTD

Characteristic	FIFO	LIFO	AVCO
• Potentially out of date valuation of inventory issues.	✓		
• The valuation of inventory rarely reflects the actual purchase price of the material.			✓
• Potentially out of date closing inventory valuation.		✓	

63   LINT LTD

Statement	True	False
• In periods of rising prices, FIFO gives a higher valuation of closing inventory than LIFO or AVCO.	✓	
• In periods of falling prices, LIFO gives a higher valuation of issues of inventory than FIFO or AVCO.		✓
• AVCO would normally be expected to produce a valuation of closing inventory somewhere between valuations under FIFO and LIFO.	✓	

64   FLUFF LTD

Characteristic	FIFO	LIFO	AVCO
• This inventory valuation method is particularly suited to inventory that consist of liquid materials e.g. oil.			✓
• This inventory valuation method is suited to inventory that has a short shelf life e.g. dairy products.	✓		
• This inventory valuation method is suited to a wheat farmer who has large silos of grain. Grain is added to and taken from the top of these silos.		✓	

65   FIDO LTD

Characteristic	FIFO	LIFO	AVCO
• In times of rising prices this method will give higher profits.	✓		
• In times of rising prices this method will give lower profits.		✓	
• In times of rising prices this method gives a middle level of profits compared to the other two.			✓

66   TRUFFEAUX LTD

Statement	True	False
• FIFO costs issues of inventory at the most recent purchase price.		✓
• AVCO costs issues of inventory at the oldest purchase price.		✓
• LIFO costs issues of inventory at the oldest purchase price.		✓
• FIFO values closing inventory at the most recent purchase price.	✓	
• LIFO values closing inventory at the most recent purchase price.		✓
• AVCO values closing inventory at the latest purchase price.		✓

67   STOCKY LTD

Characteristic	FIFO	LIFO	AVCO
• Issues are valued at the most recent purchase cost.		✓	
• Inventory is valued at the average of the cost of purchases.			✓
• Inventory is valued at the most recent purchase cost.	✓		

IDENTIFICATION OF INVENTORY VALUATION METHOD

68   EPIC LTD

Task 1

Characteristic	FIFO	LIFO	AVCO
• Closing inventory is valued at £28,200.			✓
• The issue of inventory is valued at £67,000.	✓		
• The issue of inventory is valued at £64,000.		✓	

Task 2

	True	False
• AVCO values the issue of inventory at £65,800.	✓	
• LIFO values the closing inventory at £27,000.		✓
• FIFO values the closing inventory at £30,000.		✓

69   AWESOME LTD

Task 1

Characteristic	FIFO	LIFO	AVCO
• Closing inventory is valued at £48,500.	✓		
• The issue of inventory is valued at £57,200.			✓
• The issue of inventory is valued at £66,900.		✓	

Task 2

	True	False
• FIFO values the issue of inventory at £47,500.	✓	
• AVCO values the closing inventory at £38,400.		✓
• LIFO values the closing inventory at £29,100.	✓	

70   AMAZING LTD

Task 1

Characteristic	FIFO	LIFO	AVCO
• Closing inventory is valued at £1,500.		✓	
• The issue of inventory is valued at £23,000.	✓		
• The issue of inventory is valued at £24,000.			✓

Task 2

	True	False
• LIFO values the issue of inventory at £26,500.	✓	
• AVCO values the closing inventory at £5,000.		✓
• FIFO values the closing inventory at £4,000.		✓

INVENTORY CARDS

71   STONE LTD

Method	Cost of issue on 22 June	Closing inventory at 30 June
FIFO	£10,125 (500 × £15) + (150 × £17.50)	£17,200 (£8,750 + £4,950 + £6,125 + £7,500) − £10,125
LIFO	£11,450 (275 × £18) + (350 × £17.50) + (25 × £15)	£15,875 (£8,750 + £4,950 + £6,125 + £7,500) − £11,450
AVCO	£10,732 ((£7,500 + £6,125 + £4,950)/(500 + 350 + 275)) × 650	£16,593 (£8,750 + £4,950 + £6,125 + £7,500) − £10,732

72   NATAL LTD

Task 1

Method	Cost of issue on 2 Dec	Closing inventory at 29 Dec
LIFO	£534,250 (50,000 × £7) + (14,000 × £8) + (8500 × £8.50)	£42,750 (£85,000 + £112,000 + £350,000 + £30,000) − £534,250
AVCO	£535,912 ((£85,000 + £112,000 + £350,000)/(10,000 + 14,000 + 50,000)) × 72,500	£41,088 (£85,000 + £112,000 + £350,000 + £30,000) − £535,912

Task 2

	True	False
• FIFO would give a lower closing inventory valuation on the 29th December than LIFO and AVCO.	✓	
• FIFO would give a lower cost of issue on the 25th of December than LIFO and AVCO.		✓

73   GANDALF LTD

	Valuation £
• July 15	£1,030 **(500 × £1.70) + (120 × £1.50)**
• July 31	£660 **(200 × £1.80) + (200 × £1.50)**

74   GRUNDY LTD

Method	Cost of issue on 25 October	Closing inventory at 31 October
FIFO	£20,000 **(6000 × £2.50) + (2500 × £2)**	£5,500
LIFO	£15,250 **(3000 × £1) + (3000 × £2) + (2500 × £2.50)**	£10,250
AVCO	£17,000 **(AVCO = £24,000/12000 units = £2/unit Cost of issue = 8500 × £2)**	£8,500

Tutorial note

The quickest way to calculate closing inventory is as total purchases (£25,500) less cost of issues.

75 LOBO LTD

Method	Cost of issue on 29 May	Closing inventory at 30 May
FIFO	£2,500 **(250 × £5.50) + (250 × £4.50)**	£2,250
LIFO	£1,000 **(500 × £2)**	£3,750
AVCO	£1,750 **(AVCO = £4,375/1,250 = £3.50/unit, giving cost of issue of 500 × £3.50)**	£3,000

Tutorial note

Quickest to calculate closing inventory as total purchases (£4,750) less cost of issue

76 ZOD LTD

Tutorial note

This question is harder than those seen in the sample assessment but is here to give you more of a challenge!

Method	Cost of issue on 16 Feb	Closing inventory at 26 Feb
FIFO	£290	£905
AVCO (see working below)	£255	£924

AVCO Workings:

DATE	RECEIPTS		ISSUES		BALANCE		
	Units	Cost	Units	Cost	Units	Unit cost	Total cost
February 2	100	£500			100	£5	£500
February 3			50		**(50)**	**(£5)**	**(£250)**
					50	£5	£250
February 12	150	£600			**150**	**£4**	**£600**
					200	£4.25	£850
February 16			60		**(60)**	**(£4.25)**	**(£255)**
					140	(£4.25)	£595
February 20	110	£505			**110**	£4.59 (to nearest penny)	**£505**
					250	£4.40	£1,100
February 26			40		**(40)**	**(£4.40)**	**(£176)**
					210	4.40	£924

COSTING FOR LABOUR

NARRATIVE STYLE QUESTIONS

77 NULAB LTD

Payment method	Time-rate	Piecework	Piece-rate plus bonus
• Labour is paid based on the production achieved.		✓	
• Labour is paid extra if an agreed level of output is exceeded.			✓
• Labour is paid according to hours worked.	✓		

78 LU LTD

Payment method	Time-rate	Piecework	Time-rate plus bonus
• Assured level of remuneration for employee.	✓		
• Employee earns more if they work more efficiently than expected.		✓	
• Assured level of remuneration and reward for working efficiently.			✓

79 MANDELA LTD

Statement	True	False
• Time rate is paid based on the production achieved.		✓
• Overtime is paid for hours worked over the standard hours agreed.	✓	
• Piece rate is paid according to hours worked.		✓

80 PERRES LTD

Payment method	Basic rate	Overtime premium	Overtime rate
• This is the amount paid above the basic rate for hours worked in excess of the normal hours.		✓	
• This is the total amount paid per hour for hours worked in excess of the normal hours.			✓
• This is the amount paid per hour for normal hours worked.	✓		

81 TEVEZ LTD

Statement	True	False
• Direct labour costs can be identified with the goods being made or the service being provided.	✓	
• Indirect labour costs vary directly with the level of activity.		✓

82 BERDYCH LTD

Payment method	Variable	Fixed
• Labour that is paid based on a time rate basis per hour worked.	✓	
• Labour is paid on a monthly salary basis.		✓
• Labour that is based on number of units produced.	✓	

83 SODERLING LTD

Payment method	Time-rate	Piecework	Salary
• Assured level of remuneration for employee usually agreed for the year.			✓
• Employee earnings are directly linked with units they produce.		✓	
• Employee earnings are directly linked with hours they work.	✓		

84 MURRAY LTD

	True	False
• Indirect labour costs includes production supervisors' salaries.	✓	
• Direct labour costs usually vary directly with the level of activity.	✓	

85 OWEN LTD

Payment method	Time-rate	Piecework	Salary
• Employee is paid the same amount every month.			✓
• Employee wage increases in direct correlation with the number of hours worked.	✓		
• Employee wage increases in direct correlation with the number of units produced.		✓	

86 PIECEWORK

Statement	True	False
• Piecework encourages employees to work harder.	✓	
• Piecework requires accurate recording of the number of hours staff have worked.		✓
• Piecework encourages workers to improve the quality of the units they produce.		✓

CALCULATING LABOUR COSTS

87 MUTANT LTD

Worker	Hours worked	Basic wage	Overtime	Gross wage
S. Torm	34 hours	£240	£23	£263
J. Grey	38 hours	£240	£68	£308

88 PHOENIX LTD

Statement	True	False
An employee who works 38 hours and makes 775 units will not receive a bonus.		✓
An employee who works 40 hours and makes 815 units will receive total pay of £342.50.	✓	
An employee who works 37 hours and makes 744 units will earn a bonus of £6.	✓	

89 KAHN LTD

Worker	Hours worked	Units produced	Basic wage	Bonus	Gross wage
A. Smith	35	175	£420	£0	£420
J. O'Hara	35	180	£420	£6	£426
M.Stizgt	35	185	£420	£12	£432

90 ENTERPRISE LTD

Worker	Hours worked	Basic wage	Overtime	Gross wage
J. Picard	37 hours	£420	£36	£456
B. Crusher	42 hours	£420	£126	£546
D. Troi	31 hours	£372	£0	£372

91   SGC LTD

Worker	Units produced in week	Gross wage
J. O'Neill	500 units	£660.00
S. Carter	650 units	£772.50

92   GOTHIC LTD

Worker	Hours worked	Units produced	Basic wage	Bonus	Gross wage
M. Shelley	37	300	£629	£20	£649
G. Leroux	37	312	£629	£80	£709
E. A. Poe	37	296	£629	£0	£629

93   AVENGERS LTD

Worker	Hours worked	Basic wage	Overtime	Gross wage
T. Stark	138	£1,380	£0	£1,380
B. Banner	142	£1,400	£25	£1,425
S. Rogers	145	£1,400	£63	£1,463

94   DRACO LTD

Worker	Units produced in week	Gross wage
P. Jones	240 units	£192
D. Bannatyne	350 units	£250
L. Redford	250 units	£200

95   QUAGGA PLC

Statement	True	False
During a 29 hour week, an employee producing 1,475 units would not receive a bonus.		✓
During a 32 hour week, an employee producing 1,665 units would receive a bonus of £29.25.	✓	
During a 37 hour week, an employee producing 1,925 units would receive total pay of £300.25.		✓

96   JLA PLC

Statement	True	False
During a 30 hour week, an employee producing 192 units would receive a bonus of £16.	✓	
During a 35 hour week, an employee producing 240 units would receive total pay of £215.	✓	
During a 30 hour week, an employee producing 180 units would not receive a bonus.	✓	

97   INJUSTICE LTD

Worker	Units produced	Basic wage	Piece work	Gross wage
N. Wing	295	£175	£354	£529
W. Woman	355	£175	£426	£601
T. Flash	385	£175	£462	£637

98   GREENWOOD LTD

Worker	Hours worked	Units produced	Basic wage	Bonus	Gross wage
B. Ryan	35	175	£350	£0	£350
S. Chang	35	190	£350	£21	£371
E. Schneider	35	210	£350	£49	£399

SPREADSHEETS AND VARIANCES

NARRATIVE QUESTIONS

99   VARIOUS LTD

Statement	True	False
• A variance is the difference between budgeted and actual cost.	✓	
• A favourable variance means actual costs are less than budgeted.	✓	
• An adverse variance means that actual income is less than budgeted.	✓	
• A spreadsheet can be used to store large amounts of financial information.	✓	

100 SPREADSHEETS

Identify the following statements about spreadsheets as being true or false by putting a tick in the relevant column of the table below:

Statement	True	False
• Cells are used to enter data into a spreadsheet.	✓	
• Spreadsheets cannot be protected, meaning that the data they contain is open for anyone to see.		✓
• The 'worksheet' refers to the entire spreadsheet file.		✓
• The 'sum' function is the only formula that can be used to sum a number of figures in a spreadsheet.		✓

101 STUFF LTD

Identify the following statements about spreadsheets as being true or false by putting a tick in the relevant column of the table below:

Statement	True	False
• Information can be entered into a spreadsheet either through typing it into the active cell or by entering it into the formula bar.	✓	
• All formulas have to start with an equals sign (=) to be recognized by the spreadsheet.	✓	
• Spreadsheet functions are only designed to allow users to add, subtract, multiply and divide figures.		✓
• Spreadsheets will not allow the user to display the information they contain using graphs.		✓

VARIANCE SPREADSHEET QUESTIONS

102 EREBOR LTD

Task 1

	A	B	C	D	E
1	Cost type	Budget £	Actual £	Variance £	Adverse or favourable (A or F)
2	Sales	600,500	597,800	2,700	A
3	Direct materials	205,800	208,500	2,700	A
4	Direct labour	155,000	154,800	200	F
5	Production overheads	65,000	72,100	7,100	A
6	Administration overheads	58,400	55,200	3,200	F

Task 2

	D
1	*Variance £*
2	=(B2 – C2)
3	=(B3 – C3)
4	=(B4 – C4)
5	=(B5 – C5)
6	=(B6 – C6)

Note that these formulas could be expressed in the reverse cell order (i.e. = (C2 – B2)) and this will receive full marks.

Task 3

The correct answer is **C**.

103   MORIA LTD

Task 1

	A	B	C	D	E
1	*Cost type*	*Budget*	*Variance*	*Variance as % of budget*	*Significant or Not significant*
2	Sales	45,100	4,214	9	S
3	Material	15,750	1,260	8	S
4	Labour	12,915	805	6	NS
5	Variable overheads	5,750	315	5	NS
6	Fixed overheads	8,155	1,011	12	S

Task 2

	D
1	*Variance as % of budget*
2	=C2/B2
3	=C3/B3
4	=C4/B4
5	=C5/B5
6	=C6/B6

104 WYEDALE LTD

	A	B	C	D	E	F
1	Cost type	Budget £	Actual £	Variance £	Variance %	Adverse/ Favourable
2	Sales	27,000	29,775	2,775	10	F
3	Direct materials	7,400	8,510	1,110	15	A
4	Direct labour	7,200	7,920	720	10	A
5	Production overheads	5,500	5,390	110	2	F
6	Administration overheads	4,500	4,365	135	3	F

105 BELEGOST LTD

Task 1

	A	B	C	D	E
1		Budget £	Actual £	Adverse or Favourable (A or F)	Significant or Not significant (S or NS)
2	Sales	205,000	207,100	F	NS
3	Direct materials	75,150	78,750	A	NS
4	Direct labour	110,556	107,950	F	NS
5	Production overheads	14,190	12,500	F	S
S	Non-production overheads	16,190	17,880	A	S

Task 2

	C
1	Actual
2	207,100
3	107,950
4	78,750
5	17,880
6	12,500

106 IVAN LTD

Task 1

	A	B	C	D	E
1	Cost type	Budget £	Actual £	Variance £	Adverse or favourable (A or F)
2	Sales	544,750	547,450	2,700	F
3	Direct materials	76,800	80,200	3,400	A
4	Direct labour	148,400	146,000	2,400	F
5	Production overheads	136,000	144,200	8,200	A
6	Administration overheads	105,000	109,800	4,800	A

Task 2

	D
1	Variance £
2	=B2 – C2
3	=B3 – C3
4	=B4 – C4
5	=B5 – C5
6	=B6 – C6

107 BLUEBELL LTD

Task 1

	A	B	C	D	E	F
1	Cost type	Budget £	Actual £	Variance £	Adverse/ Favourable	%
2	Sales	£204,555	£197,455	7,100	A	3
3	Direct materials	£39,000	£42,300	3,300	A	8
4	Direct labour	£75,000	£83,000	8,000	A	11
5	Production overheads	£69,000	£64,800	4,200	F	6
6	Administration overheads	£53,000	£58,900	5,900	A	11

Task 2

	F
1	*Variance* £
2	=D2/B2
3	=D3/B3
4	=D4/B4
5	=D5/B5
6	=D6/B6

SPREADSHEET FORMAT QUESTIONS

108 ELVES LTD

Task 1

Cell	Heading
C1	Fixed costs
D1	Variable costs
E1	Profit/loss

Task 2

	A	B	C	D	E
1		*Sales* (£)	*Fixed costs*	*Variable costs*	*Profit/loss*
2	January	21,000	7,500	13,300	200
3	February	24,000	7,500	15,200	1,300
4	March	18,000	7,500	11,400	−900
5	April	21,750	7,500	13,775	475
6	Total	84,750	30,000	53,675	1,075

Task 3

	A	B	C	D	E
6	Total	=sum(B2:B5)	=sum(C2:C5)	=sum(D2:D5)	=sum(E2:E5) or =B6−C6−D6

Note: Other formulas would have been acceptable. For instance, the formula in cell B6 could have been '=B2 + B3 + B4 + B5'.

109   HOBBIT PLC

Task 1

	A	B	C	D	E	F
1		Standard hours	Standard hourly rate paid (£)	Total standard pay	Bonus	Gross pay
2	Week 1	2,566	12	30,792	0	30,792
3	Week 2	3,876	12	46,512	4,651	51,163
4	Week 3	4,663	12	55,956	5,596	61,552
5	Week 4	3,445	12	41,340	0	41,340

Task 2

	D
1	Total standard pay
2	=B2*C2
3	=B3*C3
4	=B4*C4
5	=B5*C5

110   SMAUG PLC

Task 1

Cell	Heading
A2	Labour
A5	Total costs
A6	Sales

Task 2

	A	B	C	D	E
1		August	September	October	Total
2	?	13,200	24,000	18,000	55,200
3	Materials	22,000	40,000	30,000	92,000
4	Fixed overheads	5,000	5,000	5,000	15,000
5	?	40,200	69,000	53,000	162,200
6	?	38,500	70,000	52,500	161,000
7	Profit/(loss)	(1,700)	1,000	(500)	(1,200)

Task 3

	A	B	C	D	E
6	Total	=B6 – B5	=C6 – C5	=D6 – D5	=E6 – E5

Section 3

MOCK EXAM QUESTIONS

TASK 1

(a) Identify the following statements as being true or false by putting a tick in the relevant column of the table below:

Statement	True	False
• Labour paid by a simple piecework system is a variable cost.	✓	
• FIFO is a useful inventory valuation method for materials where individual units are not separately identifiable.		✓
• A cost unit is a separately identifiable part of the business where the manager is only responsible for divisional costs.		✓
• Classification of cost by behaviour is particularly useful for budgeting.	✓	

(b) Indicate whether each of the following statements regarding management accounting is true or false by putting a tick in the relevant column of the table below:

Characteristic	True	False
• Statements produced by management accounting are primarily for internal use.	✓	
• Management accounting statements are typically used to help identify the organisation's tax liability.		✓
• Management accountants produce the statement of profit or loss (income statement).		✓
• Management accounting statements normally focus on analysing past transactions.		✓

TASK 2

Morden makes and sells postcards.

(a)   **Classify the following costs by element (material, labour or overhead) by putting a tick in the relevant column of the table below:**

Cost	Material	Labour	Overheads
• Wages paid to Morden's photographer for pictures used in postcards.		✓	
• Ink used to print postcards.	✓		
• Maintenance of printers used to produce postcards.			✓
• Delivery costs to customers.			✓

Mitcham buys large rolls of wire, cuts them into various sizes and sells it on to customers.

(b)   **Classify the following costs by nature (direct or indirect) by putting a tick in the relevant column of the table below:**

Cost	Direct	Indirect
• Wages of cutting staff.	✓	
• Depreciation of cutting machinery.		✓
• Wages of the cutting staff supervisor.		✓
• Purchase of rolls of wire.	✓	

TASK 3

Bank is a company that builds houses.

(a)   **Classify the following costs by function (production, admin, selling and distribution or finance) by putting a tick in the relevant column of the table below:**

Cost	Production	Admin	Selling and distribution	Finance
• Bank charges.		✓		✓
• Purchase of bricks.	✓			
• Depreciation of office computers.		✓		
• Wages paid to advertising staff.			✓	

(b)   **Classify the following costs by behaviour (fixed, variable, semi-variable or stepped) by putting a tick in the relevant column of the table below:**

Statement	Fixed	Variable	Semi-variable	Stepped
• Purchase of plots of land to be used for building new houses.		✓		
• Hire of digging equipment. One digger is required for every 15 houses built.				✓
• Bank' total wages bill – including salaried workers as well as those paid piecework.			✓	
• Rent on Bank's head office building.	✓			

TASK 4

Cesto Plc is a supermarket and uses a coding system for its elements of cost (materials, labour or overheads) and then further classifies each element by nature (direct or indirect cost) as below. So, for example, the code for direct materials is A100.

Element of cost	Code	Nature of cost	Code
Materials	A	Direct	100
		Indirect	200
Labour	B	Direct	100
		Indirect	200
Overheads	C	Direct	100
		Indirect	200

Code the following costs, extracted from invoices and payroll, using the table below:

Cost	Code
• Purchase of milk for resale in Cesto's stores.	A100
• Wages of shelf-stackers in Cesto's stores.	B100
• Salaries of Cesto's store managers.	B200
• Public indemnity insurance.	C200
• Purchase of cleaning products for resale in Cesto's stores.	A100
• Supermarket staff canteen wages.	B200

TASK 5

FFF is a company that manufactures three different types of fizzy drink – A, B and C. It uses an alpha code for the revenue, costs or investments and then further classifies numerically as shown below:

Activity	Code	Nature of cost	Sub-code
Revenues	RE	Drink A	100
		Drink B	200
		Drink C	300
Costs	CO	Material	520
		Labour	620
		Overheads	720
Investments	IV	Drink A	100
		Drink B	200
		Drink C	300

Code the following costs, extracted from invoices and payroll, using the table below. Each transaction should have a five character code.

Cost	Code
• Investment in new machinery to manufacture Drink A.	IV100
• Wages paid to staff making Drink C.	CO620
• Sales of Drink C to Cesto Supermarkets.	RE 300
• Purchase of sugar for use in Drinks A and C.	CO 520
• Head office rental.	CO 720
• Investment in new factory for Drink C.	IV 300

TASK 6

(a) **Identify the type of cost behaviour (fixed, variable or stepped) described in each statement by putting a tick in the relevant column of the table below:**

Statement	Fixed	Variable	Stepped
• Costs are £2,000 at 3,000 to 4,000 units and £4,000 at 5,000 to 6,000 units.			✓
• Cost per unit is £5 per unit if 10,000 units are made and £10 per unit if 5,000 units are made.	✓		
• Total cost is £10,000 if 2,500 units are made and £16,000 if 4,000 units are made.		✓	

(b) **Identify the type of cost behaviour (fixed, variable or stepped) described in each statement by putting a tick in the relevant column of the table below:**

Cost	Fixed	Variable
• Salary of managing director.	✓	
• Annual cost of accounts preparation.	✓	
• Design royalty paid on every unit made.		✓

TASK 7

(a) **Identify the following costs are an overhead or not by putting a tick in the relevant column of the table below:**

Statement	Yes	No
• Depreciation of production machinery.	V	
• Fees paid for an external health and safety audit of production.	✓	✓
• Hours paid to workers on a piecework basis.		✓

Jericho Ltd makes a single product and for a production level of 16,000 units has the following cost details:

Materials   8,000 kilos at £5 per kilo   40000 = 2.50

Labour   32,000 hours at £8 an hour   256000 = 16

Fixed Overheads   £224,000

(b) **Complete the table below to show the unit cost at a REVISED production level of 20,000 units. Work to the nearest penny.**

Element	Unit cost	
Materials	£ 50000	2,50
Labour	£ 320000	16
Overheads	£ 224000	11,20
Total	£ 594000	29,70

TASK 8

(a)   Reorder the following costs into a manufacturing account format for the year ended 31 June. Use the columns to the right of the table below to enter your answer.

2	Purchases of raw materials ✓	22,000	Op. raw m.	6000
5	Direct labour V	45,000	Purch. raw	22000
12	Opening inventory of finished goods ✓	2,500	Clos. raw	(6400)
14	COST OF GOODS SOLD		Direct mat.	21600
1	Opening inventory of raw materials	6,000	Direct labor	45000
4	DIRECT MATERIALS USED ✓		Direct cost	66600
7	Manufacturing overheads V	17,000	Manuf overh.	17000
9	Opening inventory of work in progress V	4,000	Manuf. cost	83600
13	Closing inventory of finished goods	4,500	Open. WIP	4000
8	MANUFACTURING COST V		Clos. WIP	(2800)
10	Closing inventory of work in progress V	2,800	Cost manuf.	84800
3	Closing inventory of raw materials V	6,400	Open finished	2500
6	DIRECT COST V		Clos finish	(4500)
11	COST OF GOODS MANUFACTURED V		Cost sold	82800

(b)   Enter the correct figures for the following costs which were not provided in part (a).

Cost	£
DIRECT MATERIALS USED	21600
DIRECT COST	66600
MANUFACTURING COST	83600
COST OF GOODS MANUFACTURED	84800
COST OF GOODS SOLD	82800

TASK 9

Gravy Ltd carries a single type of raw material. At the start of the month, there were 25,000 litres of the material in inventory, valued at £6 per litre. During the month, Gravy bought another 50,000 litres at £3.75 per litre, followed by an issue to production of 60,000 litres at £7 per litre.

(a) **Identify the valuation method described in the statements below by putting a tick in the relevant column.**

Statement	FIFO	LIFO	AVCO
Closing inventory is valued at £67,500.			✓
The issue of inventory is costed at £281,250.	✓		
The issue of inventory is costed at £247,500.		✓	

(b) **Identify whether the statements in the table are true or false by putting a tick in the relevant column.**

Statement	True	False
• FIFO values closing inventory at £90,000.		✓
• LIFO values closing inventory at £56,250.		✓
• AVCO values the issue of inventory at £270,000.	✓	

TASK 10

Boat Ltd has the following movements in a certain type of stock into and out of it stores for the month of July.

DATE	RECEIPTS		ISSUES	
	Units	Cost	Units	Cost
July 6	350	£6,125		
July 12	500	£8,125		
July 17	150	£2,850		
July 22			400	
July 30	100	£2,000		

Complete the table below for the issue and closing stock values. Enter figures to the nearest penny.

Method	Cost of Issue on 22 July	Closing Stock at 31 July
FIFO	£ 6937.50	£ 12162.50
LIFO	£ 6912.50	£ 12187.50
AVCO	£ 6840	£ 12260

TASK 11

An employee is paid £5 per unit, and is expected to make 3 units per hour. Any work in excess of this is paid a bonus of £0.50 per unit.

(a)   **Identify the following statements as either true or false by putting a tick in the relevant column of the table below:**

Statement	True	False
• During a 31 hour working week, the employee made 92 units and did not receive a bonus.	√	
• During a 34 hour working week, the employee made 107 units and earned total pay of £537.50.	√	
• During a 25 hour week, the employee made 74 units and earned a £0.50 bonus.		√

Daft Ltd pays a time-rate of £15 per hour to its direct labour for a standard 35 hour week. Any of the labour force working in excess of 35 hours is paid an overtime rate of 'time and a half'.

(b)   **Calculate the gross wage for the week for the two workers in the table below:**

Worker	Hours worked	Basic wage	Overtime	Gross wage
S. Illy	37 hours	£ 525	£ 45	£ 570
C. Razy	43 hours	£ 525	£ 180	£ 705

TASK 12

Identify the following statements regarding labour payments as either true or false by putting a tick in the relevant column.

Statement	True	False
• An employee who is paid piecework could see a rise in their total pay if they work more hours.	√	√
• Fixed salary staff are likely to have a higher focus on quality than staff who are paid piecework.	√	
• Employees who are paid an hourly rate will earn more if they are more productive.		√
• Piecework systems enable the company to cut its wages expense if it does not need to make any more units.	√	

TASK 13

Jerry is paid £6.00 per unit produced, with a guaranteed minimum of £78 per full day he works.

Complete the table for Jerry's pay for the week

Day	Units made	Pay £
Monday	10	78
Tuesday	15	90
Wednesday	18	108
Thursday	9	78
Friday	20	120
Total weekly wage		474

TASK 14

Gassy Ltd has started the production of a spreadsheet which will enable it to calculate its profits for each month of the previous quarter.

Gassy had the following information for the four months:

Units made and sold:	April – 700
	May – 600
	June – 650
	July – 490
Variable costs	£6.00 per unit
Sales	£7.50 per unit
Fixed costs	£760 per month

	A	B	C	D	E	F
1		Sales	Variable costs	Fixed c	Tota? costs	Profit/(loss)
2	April	5,250	4,200	760	4,960	290
3	May	4500	3600	760	4360	140
4	June	4875	3900	760	4660	215
5	July	3675	2940	760	3700	-25
6	Total	18300	14640	3040	17680	620

(a)   **Decide which of the following headings should be entered into each of the cells B1, D1 and E1.**

Fixed costs

Sales

Total costs

Cell	Heading
B1	Sales
D1	Fixed
E1	Total

(b)   **Complete the table shown previously by entering the correct figures into the empty cells for rows 3 to 6 inclusive. Enter losses as negative numbers (i.e. a loss of £100 should be entered as –100)**

(c)   **Insert the formulas in the table below that you used for row 6 of columns B, C, D and F. (Note: column E is NOT required).**

	A	B	C	D	F
6	Total	=B2:B5	=C2:C5	=D2:D5	=F2:F5

TASK 15

Statement	True	False
• Spreadsheet formulas should always start with an equals sign.	✓	
• A worksheet refers to an individual page of the spreadsheet file.	✓	
• The 'ascending' function in a spreadsheet will be labeled 'A→Z'.	✓	✗
• Changing the order of lists of data is the only major function in a spreadsheet.		✓

TASK 16

Sharp Ltd has produced a performance report detailing budgeted and actual information for last month.

(a) **Calculate the amount of the variance for each cost type and enter it into the spreadsheet below. Determine whether it is adverse or favourable and put an A or F in column E.**

	A	B	C	D	E
		Budget £	Actual £	Variance £	Adverse or Favourable (A or F)
1	Cost type				
2	Sales revenue	25,550	26,888	*1338*	*F*
3	Direct labour	16,000	17,512	*1512*	*A*
4	Direct materials	2,995	2,875	*120*	*F*
5	Administration overheads	2,785	2,875	*90*	*A*
6	Selling and distribution overheads	4,100	4,298	*198*	*A*

(b) **Insert the formulas in the table below that you used in cells 2, 3, 4 and 5 of column D of the spreadsheet.**

	D
2	*=B2-C2*
3	*=B3-C3*
4	*=B4-C4*
5	*=B5-C5*

TASK 17

Shark Ltd has produced a performance report detailing budgeted and actual information for last month.

(a) **In column E identify significant variances in excess of 6% of budget, entering S for significant and NS for not significant. Variances should be calculated to two decimal places.**

	A	B	C	D	E
1	Cost type	Budget £	Actual £	Variance £	Significant or Not Significant (S or NS)
2	Sales revenue	160,000	165,400	5,400	3.38% NS
3	Direct labour	45,000	47,500	2,500 v	5.56% NS
4	Direct materials	22,700	21,200	1,500 v	6.61% S
5	Administration overheads	6,500	9,255	2,755 v	42.38% S
6	Selling and distribution overheads	25,795	27,105	1,310 v	5.08% NS

(b) **Insert the variances from column D (cells D2 to D6 inclusive) in A→Z order in the table below:**

	D
2	D6 1310
3	D4 1500
4	D3 2500
5	D5 2755
6	D2 5400

Section 4

MOCK EXAM ANSWERS

TASK 1

(a)

- True
- False
- False
- True

(b)

- True
- False
- False
- False

TASK 2

(a)

- Labour
- Material
- Overheads
- Overheads

(b)

- Direct
- Indirect
- indirect
- Direct

TASK 3

(a)

- Finance
- Production
- Admin
- Selling and distribution

(b)

- Variable
- Stepped
- Semi-variable
- Fixed

TASK 4

- A100
- B100
- B200
- C200
- A100
- B200

TASK 5

- IV100
- CO620
- RE300
- CO520
- CO720
- IV300

TASK 6

(a)

- Stepped
- Fixed
- Variable

(b)

- Fixed
- Fixed
- Variable

TASK 7

(a)

- Yes
- Yes
- No

(b)

Element	Unit cost
Materials	£2.50
Labour	£16.00
Overheads	£11.20
Total	£29.70

TASK 8

Opening inventory of raw materials	6,000	
Purchases of raw materials	22,000	
Closing inventory of raw materials	6,400	
DIRECT MATERIALS USED		
Direct labour	45,000	ɣ
DIRECT COST		
Manufacturing overheads	17,000	√
MANUFACTURING COST		
Opening inventory of work in progress	4,000	√
Closing inventory of work in progress	2,800	√
COST OF GOODS MANUFACTURED		
Opening inventory of finished goods	2,500	
Closing inventory of finished goods	4,500	
COST OF GOODS SOLD		

(b)

Cost	£
DIRECT MATERIALS USED	21,600
DIRECT COST	66,600
MANUFACTURING COST	83,600
COST OF GOODS MANUFACTURED	84,800
COST OF GOODS SOLD	82,800

TASK 9

(a)

- AVCO
- FIFO
- LIFO

(b)

- False
- False
- True

TASK 10

Method	Cost of issue on 22 July	Closing stock at 31 July
FIFO	£6,937.50	£12,162.50
LIFO	£6,912.50	£12,187.50
AVCO	£6,840.00	£12,260.00

TASK 11

(a)

- True
- True
- False

(b)

Worker	Hours worked	Basic wage	Overtime	Gross wage
S. Illy	37 hours	£525	£45	£570
C. Razy	43 hours	£525	£180	£705

TASK 12

- True
- True
- False
- True

TASK 13

Day	Units made	Pay £
Monday	10	78
Tuesday	15	90
Wednesday	18	108
Thursday	9	78
Friday	20	120
Total weekly wage		474

TASK 14

(a)

Cell	Heading
B1	Sales
D1	Fixed costs
E1	Total costs

(b)

	A	B	C	D	E	F
1		?	Variable costs	?	?	Profit/(loss)
2	April	5,250	4,200	760	4,960	290
3	May	4,500	3,600	760	4,360	140
4	June	4,875	3,900	760	4,660	215
5	July	3,675	2,940	760	3,700	−25
6	Total	18,300	14,640	3,040	17,680	620

(c)

	A	B	C	D	F
6	Total	=sum(B2:B5)	=sum(C2:C5)	=sum(D2:D5	=sum(F2:F5)

OR

	A	B	C	D	F
6	Total	=B2 + B3 + B4 + B5	=C2 + C3 + C4 + C5	=D2 + D3 + D4 + D5	=F2 + F3 + F4 + F5

TASK 15

- True
- True
- True
- False

TASK 16

(a)

	A	B	C	D	E
	Cost type	Budget £	Actual £	Variance £	Adverse or favourable (A or F)
1					
2	Sales revenue	25,550	26,888	£1,338	F
3	Direct labour	16,000	17,512	£1,512	A
4	Direct materials	2,995	2,875	£120	F
5	Administration overheads	2,785	2,875	£90	A
6	Selling and distribution overheads	4,100	4,298	£198	A

(b)

	D
1	**Variance**
2	= C2 – B2 (or = B2 – C2)
3	= C3 – B3 (or = B3 – C3)
4	= C4 – B4 (or = B4 – C4)
5	= C5 – B5 (or = B5 – C5)

TASK 17

(a)

	A	B	C	D	E
1	*Cost type*	*Budget* £	*Actual* £	*Variance* £	*Significant or Not Significant (S or NS)*
2	Sales revenue	160,000	165,400	5,400	NS
3	Direct labour	45,000	47,500	2,500	NS
4	Direct materials	22,700	21,200	1,500	S
5	Administration overheads	6,500	9,255	2,755	S
6	Selling and distribution overheads	25,795	27,105	1,310	NS

(b)

	D
2	1,310
3	1,500
4	2,500
5	2,755
6	5,400

variable and semi-variable

22,50

2,50 + 535

2,50 + 535

25000   × ₤6 =   150 000
50000   × 3,75 =   187,500   сридно ₤80
issue 60 000   × 7 =   420 000

FIFO
25000   = 150 000
35000   = 131 250
        281 250 издишан
inv. 56250

LiFO
187500
60000
247500 издишан

inv. 90000

270 000 issun

₤ 6125 + 50× 16,25 = 812,50 +   = 6937,50

2850 + 250× 16,25 = 2850 + 4062,50 =

17100 / 1000 = 17,10

17,36

AAT support

As part of your membership, you also have access to loads of other great resources to help you on your way.

→ Sign up for a MyAAT account to access exclusive services and resources.

→ Visit our social media channels for help and advice from other AAT students.

→ Check out our career support resources to get you onto the next rung of your career ladder.

→ Watch a study skills webinar event; they'll help develop your learning and ensure your study is effective.

→ Visit AAT forums for accountancy help and advice.

→ Start your full AAT membership and boost your career, job satisfaction and earnings.

→ Our interview simulator can help you prepare for your job interview increasing your chances of success.

→ Use our online CV Builder to create a CV that stands out from the crowd.

→ Interactive tutorials are online sessions that allow you to quickly gain the knowledge and skills you need.

→ Our Excel e-learning allows you to practice the skills that are relevant to you and develop your understanding of what Excel can do for you as a finance professional.

→ Look through thousands of jobs on our job search – from trainee positions through to senior management roles.

Find out more...
...about getting ready for your assessments and access to our online support materials
at **aat.org.uk/level2support**

Contents

Units

Basic costing (BCST)   6

Computerised accounting (CPAG)   8

Working effectively in accounting and finance (WKAF)   10

Processing bookkeeping transactions (PBKT)   12

Control accounts, journals and the banking system (CJBS)   14

AAT Level 2 (QCF) / Level 5 (SCQF) Certificate in Accounting

The AAT Level 2 Certificate in Accounting is the introductory level of the AAT Accounting Qualification. You'll develop your skills in finance administration: double-entry bookkeeping, basic costing principles and purchase, sales and general ledgers.

Once you've completed the introductory level, you'll be awarded the AAT Level 2 Certificate in Accounting.

A guide to help you succeed

If you're looking for a guide to help you complete your AAT Certificate in Accounting, you've come to the right place.

This guide highlights all of the study support materials available to help you complete this level and progress on to the next level. It includes the following information:

- an overview of the units
- study support available for each unit through your MyAAT account
- highlights from the *Assessment performance reports* for each unit.

Support materials are available for all units at this level – this guide helps you make best use of all the resources available to you.

Once you've looked at all of the resources, use the checklist so you can keep track of which units you've prepared for.

Basic costing
(BCST)

Overview of unit	Study support category	
→ Understanding an organisation's cost recording system and using it to record or extract data.	Guidance and standards	2
	Mapping document	1
→ Using spreadsheets to convey information on actual and budgeted income and expenditure.	E-learning	4
	Green Light test	1
	Performance feedback	1
	Sample assessment	4

Checklist

Use the checklist below to ensure you have accessed all of the support materials available for Basic costing.

Basic costing study support	✔
Standards: unit specification	☐
Guidance	☐
Mapping document	☐
Inventory valuation using AVCO e-learning module	☐
Inventory valuation using FIFO and LIFO e-learning module	☐
Actual and expected costs e-learning module	☐
Manufacturing accounts e-learning module	☐
Green Light test	☐
Assessment performance report	☐
Sample assessment (questions 1)	☐
Sample assessment answers (questions 1)	☐
Sample assessment (questions 2)	☐
Sample assessment answers (questions 2)	☐

Assessment performance feedback for Basic costing

The *Assessment performance report*, published by the Lead Assessment Writer for Basic costing, reviews student performance in all Basic costing assessments taken from 1 October 2014 to 31 March 2015. In the report, we provide task by task feedback and advice to form a comprehensive review of this unit. This includes advice on how best to approach the assessment.

The full report, including the tasks highlighted below where student performance was strong and where it was weak, is available at **aat.org.uk/level2support**

Strong performance

The task which students have performed strongest in is task 16 – Spreadsheet exercise reorganising budgeted and actual data on income and expenditure.

Nearly 90% of students either met or exceeded competence requirements, maintaining the standard reported in last year's performance report where competence achievement was the same.

Weak performance

The task which students have found most challenging is task 6 – Classification of fixed, variable and semi-variable cost.

Task 6 is divided into two parts. Student performance for this task was the same as last year with 50% of students meeting or exceeding the competence criteria. This is clearly the weakest task for student performance for the period under review and there has been little improvement from performance outcomes as reported in last year's performance review.

Have you read the Basic costing *Assessment performance report*? This is available at **aat.org.uk/level2support**

Computerised accounting
(CPAG)

Overview of unit	Study support category	

Overview of unit	Study support category	
→ Entering data at the start of an accounting period to set up customer and supplier accounts.	Guidance and standards	2
	Mapping document	1
→ Recording and processing customer and supplier transactions.	E-learning	5
→ Recording and reconciling bank and cash transactions.	Sample assessment	2
→ Processing and using journals to enter accounting transactions.		
→ Production of reports (day books, account activity, aged analysis, statements or remittance advice).		

Checklist

Use the checklist below to ensure you have accessed all of the support materials available for Computerised accounting.

Computerised accounting study support	✓
Standards: unit specification	☐
Guidance	☐
Mapping document	☐
Taking backup copies of data e-learning module	☐
Processing invoices and credit notes e-learning module	☐
How to choose a password e-learning module	☐
Entering receipts from customers e-learning module	☐
Entering opening balances e-learning module	☐
Sample assessment (questions 1)	☐
Sample assessment answers (questions 1)	☐

Akash Paul MAAT
Baker Tilly

"Everything I needed was on MyAAT. The online sample assessments were great at preparing me for the real assessments and really helped me succeed."

Working effectively in accounting and finance (WKAF)

Overview of unit	Study support category	
→ Understanding an organisation's accounting or payroll function.	Guidance and standards	2
→ Using numeracy and literacy communication skills.	Mapping document	1
→ Working independently or in a team to prioritise tasks and manage colleagues' responsibilities.	E-learning	7
→ Understanding ethical values, principles and importance of confidentiality.	Performance feedback	1
→ Understanding and explaining benefits to organisations of sustainable values.	Sample assessment	4

Checklist

Use the checklist below to ensure you have accessed all of the support materials available for Working effectively in accounting and finance.

Working effectively in accounting and finance study support	✓
Standards: unit specification	☐
Guidance	☐
Mapping document	☐
Solvency e-learning module	☐
Report writing e-learning module	☐
Conflict resolution e-learning module	☐
The accounts department e-learning module	☐
Personal development plans e-learning module	☐
Sustainability e-learning module	☐
Introduction to professional ethics e-learning module	☐
Assessment performance report	☐
Sample assessment (questions 1)	☐
Sample assessment answers (questions 1)	☐
Sample assessment (questions 2)	☐
Sample assessment answers (questions 2)	☐

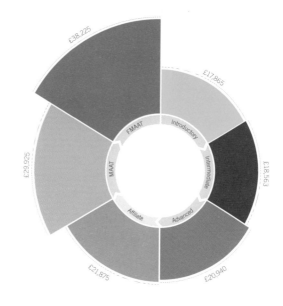

Introductory	Intermediate	Advanced	Affiliate	MAAT	FMAAT
£17,865	£18,563	£20,940	£21,875	£29,925	£38,225

*Salary ranges are from AAT's 2015 Salary Survey and represent the mean salary for people working full-time.

Mrs Tsvetelina Belstoyneva
12 Telford Drive
Walton-On-Thames
Surrey
KT12 2YH

23 February 2016

Dear Tsvetelina

We'll support you

To support you as much as we can during your AAT Level 2 Certificate in Accounting Qualification, the introductory level of the AAT Accounting Qualification, we've put together the enclosed support guide which will help you every step of the way. Enclosed you'll find the following:

AAT Level 2 Certificate in Accounting – A guide to help you succeed
This guide highlights all the support materials available to you through your MyAAT account and allows you to use a checklist to ensure you're fully prepared for each assessment. It also includes highlights from the level 2 *Assessment performance reports* – these reports will give you an understanding of how students perform at each unit.

From study support materials to study tips from other level 2 students, our resources are designed with you and your success in mind; discover these and more at **aat.org.uk/level2support**

Give your salary a boost

As you progress through the AAT Accounting Qualification, not only are you continuing on your path to a successful accounting and finance career, you could also see your salary increase. Our recent salary survey revealed that the average salary of AAT students who are studying level 2 of the AAT Accounting Qualification is £17,865*. And their salary continues to increase as they progress through the qualification and on to full membership.

If you have any questions with regards to completing your qualification, please contact our Customer Service team on **+44 (0)20 3735 2468** or by email at **membershipsupport@aat.org.uk**. Lines are open 09.00 to 17.00 (UK time), Monday to Friday.

Yours sincerely,
AAT Customer Service team

41331015 – 15,000

Member of

International
Federation
of Accountants

AAT Chief Executive: Mark Farrar. AAT is sponsored by CIPFA, ICAEW, CIMA and ICAS. A company limited by guarantee (No. 1518983) and registered as a charity (No. 1050724). Registered in England and Wales. Registered office: 140 Aldersgate Street, London, EC1A 4HY.

Assessment performance feedback for Working effectively in accounting and finance

The *Assessment performance report*, published by the Lead Assessment Writer for Working effectively in accounting and finance, reviews student performance in all Working effectively in accounting and finance assessments taken from 1 October 2014 to 31 March 2015. In the report, we provide task by task feedback and advice to form a comprehensive review of this unit. This includes advice on how best to approach the assessment.

The full report, including the tasks highlighted below where student performance was strong and where it was weak, is available at **aat.org.uk/level2support**

Strong performance

The task which students have performed strongest in is task 9 – Impact of work on others and dissatisfaction.

Task 9 is particularly well answered by the majority of students. They appear to be able to understand that the non-completion of specific tasks will impact on others. They may be assessed by being given a specific task which has not been completed and being asked to identify the impact on others within their team, the finance function or the organisation as a whole.

Weak performance

The task which students have found most challenging is task 6 – Numeracy.

Task 6 assesses the student's generic numeracy skills and is restricted to add, subtract, multiply, divide, and calculate averages, percentages, fractions, ratios and proportions. Many students find this task challenging.

Have you read the Working effectively in accounting and finance *Assessment performance report?*
This is available at **aat.org.uk/level2support**

Processing bookkeeping transactions (PBKT)

Overview of unit

→ Understanding the double-entry bookkeeping system.

→ Understanding discounts and settlement, trade and bulk discount differences.

→ Preparing and processing customer and supplier invoices and credit notes.

→ Totalling and balancing a three-column analysed cash book.

→ Totalling, balancing and reconciling petty cash records within an analysed petty cash book.

→ Processing ledger transactions and extracting a trial balance.

Study support category

Guidance and standards	2
Mapping document	1
E-learning	5
Green Light test	1
Study support webinar	2
Performance feedback	1
Sample assessment	4

Checklist

Use the checklist below to ensure you have accessed all of the support materials available for Processing bookkeeping transactions.

Processing bookkeeping transactions study support	✓
Standards: unit specification	☐
Guidance	☐
Mapping document	☐
Balancing ledger accounts e-learning module	☐
Accounting Equation and Basic Posting e-learning module	☐
Writing up sales and purchases day books e-learning module	☐
Posting from sales and sales returns day books e-learning module	☐
Posting from purchases and purchases returns day book e-learning module	☐
Green Light test	☐
Webinar recording and supporting notes	☐
Assessment performance report	☐
Sample assessment (questions 1)	☐
Sample assessment answers (questions 1)	☐
Sample assessment (questions 2)	☐
Sample assessment answers (questions 2)	☐

Assessment performance feedback for Processing bookkeeping transactions

The *Assessment performance report*, published by the Lead Assessment Writer for Processing bookkeeping transactions, reviews student performance in all Processing bookkeeping transactions assessments taken from 1 October 2014 to 31 March 2015. In the report, we provide task by task feedback and advice to form a comprehensive review of this unit. This includes advice on how best to approach the assessment.

The full report, including the tasks highlighted below where student performance was strong and where it was weak, is available at **aat.org.uk/level2support**

Strong performance

The task which students have performed strongest in is task 1 – Make entries in an analysed day-book.

Task 1 requires students to make entries into a partially completed analysed sales/sales returns/ purchases/purchases returns day-book using source documents and/or other information. Students may be required to calculate net, VAT and total amounts and to add account codes. The majority of students perform very well in this task.

Weak performance

The task which students have found most challenging is task 4 – Transfer data from a three column cash-book.

Task 4 is challenging for students and performance is the poorest of the whole assessment. Common errors include reversal of entries and selecting incorrect control accounts. Some students select a general ledger account name to record a payment or receipt in the purchases/sales ledger. However, by far the most common challenge is how the entries are affected when the cash-book is a book of prime entry only.

Have you read the Processing bookkeeping transactions *Assessment performance report?* This is available at **aat.org.uk/level2support**

Control accounts, journals and the banking system (CJBS)

Overview of unit

→ Understanding the purpose and use of control accounts and journals.

→ Maintaining and using control accounts and the journal.

→ Reconciling a bank statement with the cash book.

→ Understanding the banking process and main services of banks and building societies.

→ Understanding retention and storage requirements.

Study support category

Guidance and standards	2
Mapping document	1
E-learning	5
Green Light test	1
Study support webinar	2
Sample assessment	4

Checklist

Use the checklist below to ensure you have accessed all of the support materials available for Control accounts, journals and the banking system.

Control accounts, journals and the banking system study support	✓
Standards: unit specification	☐
Guidance	☐
Mapping document	☐
Correcting errors e-learning module	☐
Sales and Purchases Ledger Control Accounts e-learning module	☐
Wages Control Account e-learning module	☐
Analysed cash payments book e-learning module	☐
Analysed cash receipts book e-learning module	☐
Green Light test	☐
Webinar recording and supporting notes	☐
Sample assessment (questions 1)	☐
Sample assessment answers (questions 1)	☐
Sample assessment (questions 2)	☐
Sample assessment answers (questions 2)	☐